MW01484450

TALES OF WONDER
VOLUME I

THLES
Of
WONDER

WRITTEN AND COLLECTED
BY
MATTHEW GREGORY LEWIS

IN TWO VOLUMES

A NEW CRITICAL EDITION
EDITED & ANNOTATED
BY
BRETT RUTHERFORD

VOLUME I

YOGH &
THORN
BOOKS

PITTSBURGH, PENNSYLVANIA

Yogh & Thorn Edition October 2010
2nd edition, revised, March 2012
Rev 1.3 May 2017

Originally Published in Two Volumes in 1801
Notes and Annotations Copyright 2010, 2012 by Brett Rutherford

Yogh & Thorn Books are published by
THE POET'S PRESS
2209 Murray Avenue #3/ Pittsburgh, PA 15217
www.poetspress.org

This is the 196th book from The Poet's Press

ISBN 0-922558-61-2

CONTENTS

Introduction   ix

INTRODUCTION

Tales of Wonder is a landmark work in the history of Gothic literature, and a milestone in Romantic poetry. Percy Shelley owned the book as a young man, and drew ghosts and monsters in its margins; indeed, a cluster of Shelley's juvenile poems are imitations of the supernatural ballads collected here. Sir Walter Scott allowed himself to be tutored by its author and compiler, and both Scott and Robert Southey provided Gothic poems and ballads for the collection, originally to be titled *Tales of Terror*.

When the promised anthology failed to appear in due course, Scott pulled together the poems he had in hand and privately printed a sampler, titled *An Apology for Tales of Terror*. Only five copies of this 1799 book survive, and its mere existence has led some to believe, erroneously, that the *Apology* is the first edition of the present work.

Tales of Wonder was published in 1801 in two volumes in London, printed by W. Bulmer and Co., and sold by J. Bell. A second edition was issued later that year, in one volume, with Robert Southey's poems removed.[1] The single-volume second edition was the bookseller's response to complaints about the price of the two-volume set, and the inclusion, in the second volume, of many poems readily available to readers. The first Dublin printing in 1801 was the one-volume version. The two-volume version did not lack for buyers, however: an 1805 printing in Dublin, "printed for P. Wogan," is based on the two-volume original, and includes Southey's poems once again.[2]

Another book, confusingly titled *Tales of Terror*, appeared later in 1801, and as the bookseller suggested it as a suitable companion for Lewis's *Tales of Wonder*, it was mistakenly assumed by many to be Lewis's own work. The authorship of the spurious *Tales of Terror* has never been determined. The anthology contains a number of inflated parodies of supernatural ballads, alongside some that seem to be in the Lewis vein. Aside from an interesting verse *Apologia* for the Gothic that reflects contemporaneous debates about horror and The Sublime, it is otherwise a sophomoric production, perhaps intended to ridicule Lewis. Lewis seems to have ignored it, or to have quietly enjoyed the further notoriety it produced. It cost someone a good deal of money to produce, so it is not beyond the realm of possibility that Lewis participated in some way.

More than two decades ago, I came into possession of a dog-eared copy of Henry Morley's 1887 compilation, titled *Tales of Terror and*

---

[1] "There is a sort of Imbroglio about Southey's ballads, which must be settled," Lewis wrote to Walter Scott (Peck 119).

[2] Louis Peck notes an 1817 edition in London with 32 poems, an 1836 edition with only 23, and a 1925 "catchpenny" edition with only eight poems (133).

Wonder. Morley cobbled together the Lewis original with the spurious *Tales of Terror*, and, where pages were missing from his copies of the two books, he simply omitted those poems. Morley's introductory essay has so many rabbit holes of error that it is best not to read it, nor to torment others by citing it.

My original intent, when embarking on this project, was simply to find Lewis's first edition and to make it available once again.

At first glance, many of these poems seem to be works of pure imagination. Many occupy a Gothic realm of knights, libidinous monks, devils and witches, ravished damsels and haunted woods. Once I had determined to annotate the poems, however — intending to limit myself to defining arcane words for today's students or general readers — I discovered that many of these poems have a deep history, rooted not only in their literary sources but also in specific times and places. My intertextual detective work has sought out alternate tellings of the narrative in these poems, in some cases finding the actual source, one dating back to 300 BCE.

The research into these poems also introduced me to the work of several generations of scholars who collected Runic poetry and English and Scottish ballads. These eccentrics — some clerics and some gentlemen with the income and inclination to explore monastery libraries or transcribe Runic stone carvings — were at work in a serious intellectual project: to ground Britain in an alternate pre-history that was neither Biblical nor Greco-Roman. This pagan yearning for Icelandic and Danish and Saxon literary and historical roots, is celebrated in some of the poems in this book. Although there are no dour Druids here, the lore of Wotan/Odin and the sombre epics of the North figure large.

The annotations in this new edition document the origins of the poems Lewis translated or selected. In some cases, I have inserted alternate translations or originals; in others I am content to point interested readers to the sources. The great mother lode of English and Scottish ballads can be found in Bishop Percy's *Reliques of Ancient English Poetry*, LeGrand's *Fabliaux*, and Evans' *A Collection of Old Ballads*. Child's *English and Scottish Popular Ballads*, although published later in the century (starting in 1868), is also cited frequently in the notes, since the Child ballad collection is comprehensive and the numbering of the ballads therein has become a standard cataloging reference.

It should not be forgotten that the literary ballad, where it is not a complete invention, is fossil evidence of a work intended to be sung, and accompanied by some kind of instrument. Some supernatural ballads were also transmitted in broadsheets and printed collections, often with musical notation. Ballad-singing was a tea-time entertainment, and sophisticated settings of such ballads by Haydn and Beethoven kept the text of the ballad in the public eye as song lyrics. The leap from folk-lyric to literary ballad set a higher standard for the ballad-as-text, and Lewis and his peers made it their business to add metric regularity and poetic diction into the sometimes rougher-hewn originals. Sometimes the texts are Anglicised or modernized; other times a new-fangled poem is cast in archaic language, either for atmosphere or as an outright literary hoax.

These editors, who collected ballads from oral transmission, also stood on the shoulders of monks and chroniclers who passed along, in Latin, wonderful tall tales such as "The Old Woman of Berkeley." One approaches these ballad compilations with awe and caution commingled: some of the poets in this collection were involved in the creation of mock ballads that passed back into the literature.

Now that this first of two volumes is in hand, it is possible to step back and look at the remarkable range of work Lewis has assembled, skewed as the first volume is with the compiler's eagerness to put his own work forward. Here we are treated to a ghost/vampire tale first penned around 300 BCE; a Runic funeral song from the tenth century CE; a meeting between the Saxon invader of England and a Roman ghost; a Nordic warrior woman's incantation to raise her father from the dead; Goethe's blood-curdling multi-voiced "Erl-King" and fatal water nymphs; the monk and nun who try (unsuccessfully) to save their witch mother from the Devil; a proud painter's encounters with Satan; a doomed romance set in the horrific landscape of the War of the Spanish Succession; and the endless forest ride of "The Wild Huntsmen." (In the second volume, the reader will encounter work by Burns, Dryden, Jonson, Gray, and Bürger, as well as items from the Percy and Evans collections of old ballads.)

One caveat for the reader weaned on modern poetry is that even the "Romantic" poets featured here employ forms, meters and language from an era earlier than their own, even sometimes to the extent of perpetrating a literary hoax à la Ossian. The Gothic esthetic by its nature is backward-looking. It takes some adjustment for today's reader to enjoy these poems for what they are, and read them in the context of their own time. Against the stifling moral and correct tone of most 18th century verse, this is pretty strong stuff, a bracing counter-esthetic.

We need also remember that Lewis — whose Gothic plays shocked and appalled London audiences, and whose lurid novel, *The Monk*, mixed sex and demon possession — invested much in this book. Far more than just self-promotion of his own Gothic verses, the range of material selected demonstrates the unbroken interest in the weird and wonderful stretching back to antiquity.

A certain degree of macabre relish, what I call "the smile behind the skull," is also evident throughout. The poems here are unlikely to frighten anyone other than the superstitious, or very small children; instead, they delight those of a Gothic predilection who enjoy the sublime frisson of danger and supernatural awe. The tone of this book sets the mode for erudition, arcane allusion, atmosphere and devastation — with a dose of *Grand Guignol* humor for the initiate — that we will see later in Edgar Allan Poe and H.P. Lovecraft. Lovecraft would have recognized Lewis and the antiquarian eccentrics whose work anticipates Gothic poetry, as brothers.

I would like to acknowledge Lance Arney, who many years ago undertook the task of typing the 1887 *Tales of Terror and Wonder* into a computer. He raised the question of whether some of the poems in that edition were so absurd as to be parodies, and, as it turned out, he was correct.

In one of those delightful (or dismaying) coincidences of publishing, my first edition of Volume I of *Tales of Wonder* was published in October 2010, and Broadview Editions issued its own *Tales of Wonder*, edited by Douglass H. Thomson, the same month. I had not been familiar with any of Dr. Thomson's remarkable work except his research, published online, into the Walter Scott *Apology for Tales of Terror*, to which I had referred readers. Thomson's masterful introduction and notes go into great depth about the place of Lewis's work in the development of Gothic romanticism, and he devotes many pages to the problem of parody in the supernatural poems Lewis wrote and chose. Although he limits himself to Volume I and selections from Volume II, and a few selections from the spurious *Tales of Terror*, Thomson's edition is indispensable for scholars.

My somewhat different focus requires the republication and annotation of both volumes, as Lewis presented them in 1801, illuminated by a study of the textual and narrative sources of the poems, and such information about the poets as will shed light on the interpretation of the text. I am also undaunted by the "tales of plunder" accusation against Lewis for using already-familiar poems and ballads, since most of the texts presented here will be new to today's reader. My aim in this two-volume edition is to serve the educated general reader (whose existence I still believe in) as well as the academic. Happily, since this project is published in print and in ebook format with today's "on demand" printing, I can continue to revise *Tales of Wonder* as new information comes to hand.

I hope that this new edition of the real *Tales of Wonder* will help restore Matthew Gregory Lewis to his rightful place in the history of Gothic literature and of Romanticism. Although biographers of Mary Shelley have made note of "Monk" Lewis's visit to the Villa Deodati in 1816, and the sharing ghost stories among Lewis, Lord Byron, Dr. Polidori, and Percy and Mary Shelley, none seem to have realized who among them had the most to say about the writing of a ghost story.

I am delighted that *Tales of Wonder* is finally coming into its own.

—*Brett Rutherford*
University of Rhode Island
October 10, 2010/ February 19, 2012

ANNOTATIONS AND SOURCES

All of the unattributed annotations in this book are my own. The original footnotes by Lewis are marked as "—MGL," and I have availed myself of Sir Walter Scott's 1833 annotations to his own poetry, marking those "—WS." I have added my initials to annotations only on those occasions where mine are interspersed with those of others, or where I wanted to make clear that a certain note was *not* by Lewis or one of the poets. I welcome correspondence from readers and scholars, and would be pleased to correct or elaborate on any of the notes should new information come to light. As the great Cuvier wrote: "An error corrected is new knowledge."

The 32 items identified in the Table of Contents with large Roman numerals correspond to the items originally published in Volume I of *Tales of Wonder.* The indented items in the Table of Contents comprise the source documents, alternate texts and additional notes. None of these source materials were in Lewis's 1801 edition, nor in any subsequent edition.

TALES OF WONDER

BOTHWELL CASTLE.

Bothwell's Bonny Jane

M. G. LEWIS

Bothwell Castle is beautifully situated upon the Clyde, and fronts the ruins of Blantyre Priory[1]. The estate of Bothwell has long been, and continues to be, in the possession of the Douglas family.[2]

Loud roars the north round Bothwell's hall,
    And fast descends the pattering rain:
But streams of tears still faster fall
    From thy blue eyes, oh! bonny Jane!

Hark! hark! — I hear, with mournful yell,
    The wraiths[3] of angry Clyde complain;
But sorrow bursts with louder swell
    From thy fair breast, oh! bonny Jane!

"Tap! — tap!" — who knocks? —the door unfolds;
    The mourner lifts her melting eye,
And soon with joy and hope beholds
    A reverend monk approaching nigh:

His air is mild, his step is slow,
    His hands across his breast are laid,
And soft he sighs, while bending low,
    "St. Bothan[4] guard thee, gentle maid!"

To meet the friar the damsel ran;
    She kissed his hand, she clasped his knee.
—"Now free me, free me, holy man,
    Who com'st from Blantyre Prio-rie!"

---

[1] *Blantyre Priory.* Established in 1296 AD and abandoned by the 1600s.
[2] Lewis was a guest at Bothwell Castle in December 1793.
[3] *Wraiths.* Water-spirits —MGL.
[4] *St. Bothan.* The patron saint of Bothwell —MGL.

<17>

— "What mean these piteous cries, daughter?
    St. Bothan be thy speed!
Why swim in tears thine eyes, daughter?
    From whom would'st thou be freed?" —

— "Oh! father, father! know, my sire,
    Though long I knelt, and wept, and sigh'd,
Hath sworn, ere twice ten days expire,
    His Jane shall be Lord Malcolm's bride!" —

"Lord Malcolm is rich and great, daughter, —
    And comes of a high degree;
He's fit to be thy mate, daughter,
    So, *Benedicite*[5]!" —

— "Oh! father, father! say not so!
    Though rich his halls, though fair his bowers, —
There stands a hut, where Tweed doth flow,
    I prize beyond Lord Malcolm's towers:

"There dwells a youth where Tweed doth glide,
    On whom nor rank, nor fortune smiles;
I'd rather be that peasant's bride,
    Than reign o'er all Lord Malcolm's isles." —

— "But should you flee away, daughter,
    And wed with a village clown,
What would your father say, daughter?
    How would he fume and frown!"

— "Oh! he might frown and he might fume,
    And Malcolm's heart might grieve and pine,
So Edgar's hut for me had room,
    And Edgar's lips were pressed to mine!" —

---

[5] *Benedicite*. Latin: Bless you.

<18>

— "If at the castle gate, daughter,
    At night, thy love so true
Should with a courser⁶ wait, daughter, . . .
    What, daughter, would'st thou do?" —

— "With noiseless step the stairs I'd press,
    Unclose the gate, and mount with glee,
And ever, as on I sped, would bless
    The abbot of Blantyre Prio-rie!" —

— "Then, daughter, dry those eyes so bright;
    I'll haste where flows Tweed's silver stream
And when thou see'st, at dead of night,
    A lamp in Blantyre's chapel gleam,

"With noiseless step the staircase press,
    For know, thy lover there will be;
Then mount his steed, haste on, — and bless
    The abbot of Blantyre Prio-rie!" —

Then forth the friar he bent his way,
    While lightly danc'd the damsel's heart;
Oh! how she chid the length of day,
    How sighed to see the sun depart!

How joyed she when eve's shadows came,
    How swiftly gained her towers so high! —
— "Does there in Blantyre shine a flame?
    Ah! no — the moon deceived mine eye!" —

Again the shades of evening lour;
    Again she hails the approach of night.
— "Shines there a flame in Blantyre tower?
    Ah! no — 'tis but the northern light!⁷" —

---

⁶ *Courser.* A fast horse, fit for racing or a rapid escape from pursuers.
⁷ *Northern light.* The Aurora Borealis.

<19>

But when arriv'd All-hallow E'en[8],
    What time the night and morn divide,
The signal-lamp by Jane was seen
    To glimmer on the waves of Clyde.

She cares not for her father's tears,
    She feels not for her father's sighs;
No voice but headstrong Love's she hears,
    And down the staircase swift she hies.

Though thrice the Brownie[9] shrieked — "Beware!" —
    Though thrice was heard a dying groan,
She oped the castle gate. — Lo! there
    She found the friendly monk alone.

— "Oh! where is Edgar, father, say?" —
    — "On! on!" the friendly monk replied;
"He feared his berry-brown steed should neigh,
    "And waits us on the banks of Clyde."

Then on they hurried, and on they hied,
    Down Bothwell's slope so steep and green,
And soon they reached the river's side —
    Alas! no Edgar yet was seen!

Then, bonny Jane, thy spirits sunk;
    Filled was thy heart with strange alarms!
— "Now thou art mine!" exclaimed the monk,
    And clasp'd her in his ruffian arms.

---

[8] *All-hallow E'en*. On this night witches, devils, &c., are thought, by the Scotch, to be abroad on their baneful errands. See Burns' poem, under the title of "Hallowe'en."—MGL [The all-pervasive pagan holiday of Hallowe'en (Samhain) was so little known in Lewis's time that it required a footnote! Before Fraser's *The Golden Bough* and its revelations, the Christian mythos had almost completely obscured the origins of Hallowe'en as the eve of the Druid New Year—BR].

[9] *Brownie*. The *Brownie* is a domestic spirit, whose voice is always heard lamenting, when any accident is about to befall the family to which she has attached herself —MGL.

<20>

"Know, yonder bark must bear thee straight,
    Where Blantyre owns my gay control:
There Love and Joy to greet thee wait,
    There Pleasure crowns for thee her bowl.

"Long have I loved thee, bonny Jane,
    Long breathed to thee my secret vow!
Come then, sweet maid! — nay, strife is vain;
    Not heaven itself can save thee now!"

The damsel shrieked, and would have fled,
    When lo! his poniard[10] pressed her throat!
— "One cry, and 'tis your last" he said,
    And bore her fainting tow'rds the boat.

The moon shone bright; the winds were chained;
    The boatman swiftly plied his oar;
But ere the river's midst was gained,
    The tempest-fiend was heard to roar.

Rain fell in sheets; high swelled the Clyde;
    Blue flamed the lightning's blasting brand!
— "Oh! lighten the bark!" the boatman cried,
    "Or hope no more to reach the strand.

"E'en now we stand on danger's brink!
    E'en now the boat half filled I see!
Oh! lighten it soon, or else we sink!
    Oh! lighten it of . . . your gay la-die!"

With shrieks the maid his counsel hears;
    But vain are now *her* prayers and cries,
Who cared not for her father's tears,
    Who felt not for her father's sighs!

---

[10] *Poniard.* A dagger.

<21>

Fear conquer'd love! — In wild despair
    The abbot view'd the watery grave,
Then seized his victim's golden hair,
    And plunged her in the foaming wave!

She screams! — she sinks! —"Row, boatman, row!
    The bark is light!" the abbot cries;
"Row, boatman, row to land!" — When lo!
    Gigantic grew the boatman's size!

With burning steel his temples bound
    Throbbed quick and high with fiery pangs;
He rolled his blood-shot eyeballs round,
    And furious gnash'd his iron fangs;

His hands two gore-fed scorpions grasp'd;
    His eyes fell joy and spite express'd.
— "Thy cup is full!" he said, and clasped
    The abbot to his burning breast.

With hideous yell down sinks the boat,
    And straight the warring winds subside;
Moon-silvered clouds through aether float,
    And gently murmuring flows the Clyde.

Since then full many a winter's powers
    In chains of ice the earth have bound;
And many a spring, with blushing flowers
    And herbage gay, has robed the ground:

Yet legends say, at Hallow-E'en,
    When Silence holds her deepest reign,
That still the ferryman-fiend is seen
    To waft the monk and bonny Jane:

<22>

And still does Blantyre's wreck display
    The signal-lamp at midnight hour;
And still to watch its fatal ray,
    The phantom fair haunts Bothwell Tower;

Still tunes her lute[11] to Edgar's name[12],
    Still chides the hours which stay her flight;
Still sings — "In Blantyre shines the flame?
    Ah! no! — 'tis but the northern light!"

---

[11] *Lute*. Medieval plucked string instrument, still in use in the early 1700s; largely replaced by the mandolin and guitar. The lute remained a staple in Gothic literature, and is the instrument played by Roderick Usher in Edgar Allan Poe's *The Fall of the House of Usher*. The lute has enjoyed a revival as a result of the early music movement.

[12] *Tunes her lute to Edgar's name*. There may be a word-play here since the name "Edgar" contains the four musical notes E, D, G, and A.

<23>

Osric the Lion

M. G. LEWIS

Since writing this Ballad, I have seen a French one, entitled "La Veillée de la Bonne Mère," which has some resemblance with it.[1]

Swift roll the Rhine's billows, and water the plains,
Where Falkenstein Castle's[2] majestic remains
    Their moss-covered turrets still rear:
Oft loves the gaunt wolf 'midst the ruins to prowl,
What time from the battlements pours the lone owl
    Her plaints in the passenger's ear.

No longer resound through the vaults of yon hall
The song of the minstrel, and mirth of the ball;
    Those pleasures for ever are fled:
There now dwells the bat with her light-shunning brood,
There ravens and vultures now clamour for food,
    And all is dark, silent, and dread!

Ha! dost thou not see, by the moon's trembling light
Directing his steps, where advances a knight,
    His eye big with vengeance and fate?
'Tis Osric the Lion[3] his nephew who leads,
And swift up the crackling old staircase proceeds,
    Gains the hall, and quick closes the gate.

---

[1] Lewis had in mind Jacques Cazotte's 1753 poem, "Tout au beau milieu des Ardennes, ou La Veillée de la bonne femme," a proto-Gothic ballad replete with demons and ghosts in a haunted castle. Cazotte was a prolific writer of fables, fairy tales, and Oriental pastiches.
[2] *Falkenstein Castle* (Burg Falkenstein), "Falcon-Stone," originally *Castrum Pfronten*, is a castle-ruin in the Bavarian Alps. It is the highest castle in Germany, built between 1270 and 1280 CE.
[3] *Osric the Lion*. Lewis mixes Anglo-Saxon and German names in this poem. According to The *Anglo-Saxon Chronicle*, Osric was a ruler of Northumbria (718-729 CE). Another Osric, King of Sussex, died in 915 CE.

<25>

Now round him young Carloman[4] casting his eyes,
Surveys the sad scene with dismay and surprise,
    And fear steals the rose from his cheeks.
His spirits forsake him, his courage is flown;
The hand of Sir Osric he clasps in his own,
    And while his voice falters he speaks.

— "Dear uncle," he murmurs, "Why linger we here?
'Tis late, and these chambers are damp and are drear,
    Keen blows through the ruins the blast!
Oh! let us away and our journey pursue:
Fair Blumenberg's Castle[5] will rise on our view,
    Soon as Falkenstein forest is passed.

"Why roll thus your eyeballs? why glare they so wild?
Oh! chide not my weakness, nor frown, that a child
    Should view these apartments with dread;
For know, that full oft have I heard from my nurse,
There still on this castle has rested a curse,
    Since innocent blood here was shed.

"She said, too, bad spirits, and ghosts all in white,
Here used to resort at the dead time of the night,
    Nor vanish till breaking of day;
And still at their coming is heard the deep tone
Of a bell loud and awful — hark! Hark! 'twas a groan!
    "Good uncle, oh! let us away!" —

---

4 *Carloman*. A royal name: King Carloman (d. 771 CE) the son of Charles
Martel, was succeeded by his son Charlemagne. This poem probably refers,
however, to Carloman, King of Bavaria from 877 to 880 CE.
5 *Blumenberg* is a mountain peak near Eichstädt, Bavaria. Eichstädt is the home
of the Catholic University of Eichstädt-Ingolstadt, the first Bavarian University,
founded in 1472. In Mary Shelley's *Frankenstein*, the hero travels to this
university to conduct his studies. Was this poem one of the "ghost stories" Lewis
shared with his hosts during his visit to the Shelleys, Byron and Dr. Polidori in
the summer of 1816? One hastens to add that there is no "castle" in Mary
Shelley's novel: the monster is created in Victor Frankenstein's student lodgings
in Ingolstadt.

<26>

— "Peace, serpent!" thus Osric the Lion replies,
While rage and malignity gloom in his eyes;
    "Thy journey and life here must close:
Thy castle's proud turrets no more shalt thou see;
No more betwixt Blumenberg's lordship and me
    Shalt thou stand, and my greatness oppose.

"My brother lies breathless on Palestine's plains,
And thou once removed, to his noble domains
    My right can no rival deny:
Then, stripling, prepare on my dagger to bleed;
No succour is near, and thy fate is decreed,
    Commend thee to Jesus, and die!" —

Thus saying, he seizes the boy by the arm,
Whose grief rends the vaulted hall's roof, while alarm
    His heart of all fortitude robs;
His limbs sink beneath him; distracted with fears,
He falls at his uncle's feet, bathes them with tears,
    And — "spare me! oh, spare me!" — he sobs.

But vainly the miscreant he strives to appease;
And vainly he clings in despair round his knees,
    And sues in soft accents for life;
Unmoved by his sorrow, unmoved by his prayer,
Fierce Osric has twisted his hand in his hair,
    And aims at his bosom a knife.

But ere the steel blushes with blood, strange to tell!
Self-struck, does the tongue of the hollow-toned bell
    The presence of midnight declare:
And while with amazement his hair bristles high,
Hears Osric a voice, loud and terrible, cry,
    In sounds heart-appalling — "Forbear!"

<27>

Straight curses and shrieks through the chambers resound,
Shrieks mingled with laughter: the walls shake around;
    The groaning roof threatens to fall;
Loud bellows the thunder, blue lightnings still flash;
The casements they clatter; chains rattle; doors clash,
    And flames spread their waves through the hall.

The clamour increases, the portals expand! —
O'er the pavement's black marble now rushes a band
    Of demons, all dropping with gore,
In visage so grim, and so monstrous in height,
That Carloman screams, as they burst on his sight,
    And sinks without sense on the floor.

Not so his fell uncle: — he sees, that the throng
Impels, wildly shrieking, a female along,
    And well the sad spectre he knows!
The demons with curses her steps onward urge;
Her shoulders, with whips formed of serpents, they scourge,
    And fast from her wounds the blood flows.

<28>

"Oh! welcome!" she cried, and her voice spoke despair;
"Oh! welcome, Sir Osric, the torments to share,
  Of which thou hast made me the prey.
Twelve years have I languished thy coming to see;
Ulrilda, who perished dishonoured by thee,
  Now calls thee to anguish away!

"Thy passion once sated, thy love became hate;
Thy hand gave the draught which consigned me to fate,
  Nor thought I death lurked in the bowl:
Unfit for the grave, stained with lust, swelled with pride,
Unblessed, unabsolved, unrepenting, I died,
  And demons straight seized on my soul.

"Thou com'st, and with transport I feel my breast swell:
Full long have I suffer'd the torments of hell,
  And now shall its pleasures be mine!
See, see, how the fiends are athirst for thy blood!
Twelve years has *my* panting heart furnished their food,
  Come, wretch, let them feast upon thine!" —

She said, and the demons their prey flocked around;
They dashed him, with horrible yell, on the ground,
  And blood down his limbs trickled fast;
His eyes from their sockets with fury they tore;
They fed on his entrailes, all reeking with gore,
  And his *heart* was Ulrilda's repast.

But now the grey cock told the coming of day!
The fiends with their victim straight vanished away,
  And Carloman's heart throbbed again;
With terror recalling the deeds of the night,
He rose, and from Falkenstein speeding his flight,
  Soon reached his paternal domain.

<29>

Since then, all with horror the ruins behold;
No shepherd, though strayed be a lamb from his fold,
    No mother, though lost be her child,
The fugitive dares in these chambers to seek,
Where fiends nightly revel, and guilty ghosts shriek
    In accents most fearful and wild!

Oh! shun them, ye pilgrims! though late be the hour,
Though loud howl the tempest, and fast fall the shower;
    From Falkenstein Castle be gone!
There still their sad banquet hell's denizens share;
There Osric the Lion still raves in despair:
    Breathe a prayer for his soul, and pass on!

<30>

Sir Ḣengist

German. M. G. LEWIS

Hermann, or Arminius[1], is the favourite hero of Germany, whose liberty he defended against the oppression of Rome: Flavus, his brother, sided with the Romans, and in consequence his memory is as much detested by his countrymen as that of Arminius is beloved. — I forget where I met the original of this Ballad[2].

Where rolls the Weser's[3] golden sand,
Did erst Sir Hengist's[4] castle stand,
   A warrior brave and good;
His lands extended far and wide,
Where streamed full many a plenteous tide,
   Where frowned full many a wood.

---

[1] *Arminius* (c. 18 BCE – 21 CE), led an array of Germanic tribes in battles against Roman armies, including the infamous Battle of Teutoberg Forest (9 CE), the greatest defeat ever suffered by Rome. The captured Romans were butchered and ritually sacrificed. At various times, Arminius or "Hermann" has been offered as the original model of Sigurd or Siegfried, and monuments to Arminius have been raised both in Germany and abroad.

[2] *Original*. There may not be an original from German or Danish. The poem's use of a British proto-founder encountering the ghost of Flavus makes it suspiciously British in origin, and very much a late 18th-century product of English Gothic enthusiasm. Lewis may be playing Ossian here, *i.e.*, attempting a literary hoax, an attempt at Saxon-Roman synthesis.

[3] *Weser*. The longest river contained entirely in Germany, beginning at Hann. Münden and flowing north to Bremen on the North Sea. The references to "sand" and "tide" suggest that Hengist's castle is near the mouth of the river, not inland.

[4] *Hengist*. A Saxon name. Bede refers to Hengist and Horsa, as great-grand-children of "Uoden," in *Historia Ecclesiastica I:15*. Hengist and his brother Horsa led the 5th Century Anglo-Saxon-Jute invasion of Britain. Hengist's exploits are given imaginative elaboration in Geoffrey of Monmouth's *Historia Regum Britanniae* (1136 CE). Hengist and Horsa, the "horse brothers," occupy a parallel space in the British mythos to Romulus and Remus, brothers suckled by a wolf mother.

<31>

It chanced, that homewards from the chase
Sir Hengist urged his courser's pace,
 The shadowy dales among,
While all was still, and late the hour,
And far off, in the castle tower,
 The bell of midnight rung.

Sudden a piercing shriek resounds
Throughout the forest's ample bounds;
 A wildly dreadful yell;
The dogs, by trembling, own their fear,
As if they scent some bad thing near,
 Some soul enlarged from hell!

— "See, father!" cried young Egbert[5]; "see
Beneath the shade of yonder tree
 What fearful form is spread!
How fire around his temples glows!
How from his lance and fingers flows
 The stream of bloody red!"

— "Stay here!" said Hengist, then with speed
Towards the stranger spurred his steed;
 "What brings thee here, Sir Knight,
Who darest in my domains to bear
A lance, and by thy haughty air
 Seem'st to demand the fight?" —

— "Long has my arm forgot to wield
The sword, and raise the massy shield,"
 Replied the stranger drear:
"Peace to this brown oak's hallowed shade!
Peace to the bones which here are laid,
 And which we both revere!

---

[5] *Egbert. The Anglo Saxon Chronicle* for the year 455 refers to Hengist's son as "Esc."

<32>

Odin rides to Hel.

"Know'st thou not Siegmar[6], Herman's sire,
That arm of steel, that soul of fire?
   Here is his grave. — My name
Is Flavus[7] — at that sound the woods
With curses ring, and Weser's floods
   My infamy proclaim!

"For such is vengeful Odin's[8] will
And doom, that traitor-curses still
   Thick on my head shall be,
Till from the blood of brethren slain,
My gory hands and lance again
   I pure and spotless see.

[6] *Siegmar*. Segimerus, chieftain of the Cheruscan German tribe.
[7] *Flavus*. Brother or brother-in-law of Arminius. Flavus means "yellow" in Latin, and may have been a reference to blond hair.
[8] *Odin*. Norse equivalent of Wotan, king of the gods.

<33>

Hengist and Horsa. "The Arrival of the First Ancestors of Englishmen out of Germany into Britain," from *A Restitution of Decayed Intelligence* by Richard Verstegan (1605).

<34>

"Still then, when midnight hours permit
Pale spectres Hela's[9] realm to quit,
 I seek this hallowed place;
With tears bedew these crimson blots,
And strive to wash away the spots
 No pains can now efface!"

He ceased; when Odin's eagle came,
By Odin armed with blasting flame,
 And seized the phantom knight:
Loud shrieks the spectre's pangs reveal'd,
And soon a cloud his form concealed
 From awe-struck Hengist's sight.

— "Son!" said the chief, with horror chill'd,
While down his brows cold dews distill'd,
 "Now take your sword in hand,
And swear with me, each drop of gore,
That swells your veins, well pleased to pour
 To guard your native land!"

---

[9] *Hela*. In Norse Myth, Hel is the realm of the dead, akin to The Greek Hades as a universal destination after death, not a place of punishment. The ruler of Hel, also named "Hel," is female, and Lewis may have feminized her name here. Thomas Gray precedes Lewis in this usage: "Hela" is named in his poem, "The Descent of Odin." (*Poems by Mr. Gray*, 1768, p. 49). Hela also suggests Mt. Hekla in Iceland, a volcano widely believed since the 12th century to contain the entrance to Hell.

<35>

Alonzo the Brave and Fair Imogene

Original. — M. G. LEWIS

This was first published in the third volume of Ambrosio, or the Monk.[1]

A warrior so bold and a virgin so bright
    Conversed, as they sat on the green;
They gazed on each other with tender delight:
Alonzo the Brave was the name of the knight,
    The maid's was the Fair Imogene.

— "And, oh!" said the youth, "since to-morrow I go
    To fight in a far distant land,
Your tears for my absence soon leaving to flow,
Some other will court you, and you will bestow
    On a wealthier suitor your hand."

— "Oh! hush these suspicions," Fair Imogene said,
    "Offensive to love and to me!
For, if you be living, or if you be dead,
I swear by the Virgin, that none in your stead
    Shall husband of Imogene be.

"And if e'er for another my heart should decide,
    Forgetting Alonzo the Brave,
God grant, that, to punish my falsehood and pride,
Your ghost at the marriage may sit by my side,
May tax me with perjury, claim me as bride,
    And bear me away to the grave!" —

---

[1] The poem was adapted into an elaborate ballet, *Alonzo and Imogine; or The Bridal Spectre*, at Sadler's Wells in 1797 and a pantomime at Covent Garden by H.M. Milner, with dancing sekletons and a flying tomb. In 1801, another ballet adaptation titled *A Grand Ballet of Alonzo the Brave and the Fair Imogene* was performed at the Haymarket and at Drury Lane. The appetite for Gothic stage thrills seems to have been enormous (Peck 32).

<36>

To Palestine hastened the hero so bold;
   His love she lamented him sore:
But scarce had a twelvemonth elapsed, when behold,
A Baron all covered with jewels and gold
   Arrived at Fair Imogene's door.

His treasure, his presents, his spacious domain,
   Soon made her untrue to her vows:
He dazzled her eyes; he bewildered her brain;
He caught her affections so light and so vain,
   And carried her home as his spouse.

And now had the marriage been blessed by the priest;
   The revelry now was begun:
The tables they groaned with the weight of the feast;
Nor yet had the laughter and merriment ceased,
   When the bell of the castle toll'd — "one!"

Then first with amazement Fair Imogene found
   That a stranger was placed by her side:
His air was terrific; he uttered no sound;
He spoke not, he moved not, he looked not around,
   But earnestly gazed on the bride.

His vizor was closed, and gigantic his height;
   His armour was sable to view;
All pleasure and laughter were hushed at his sight;
The dogs, as they eyed him, drew back in affright;
   The lights in the chamber burnt blue!

His presence all bosoms appeared to dismay;
   The guests sat in silence and fear:
At length spoke the bride, while she trembled — "I pray,
Sir Knight, that your helmet aside you would lay,
   And deign to partake of our cheer." —

<37>

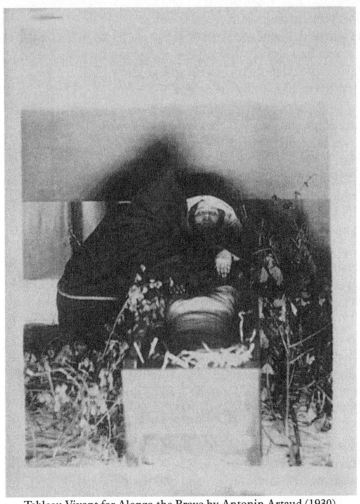

Tableau Vivant for Alonzo the Brave by Antonin Artaud (1930).

The lady is silent: the stranger complies,
    His vizor he slowly unclosed;
Oh! then what a sight met Fair Imogene's eyes!
What words can express her dismay and surprise,
    When a skeleton's head was exposed!

<38>

All present then uttered a terrified shout;
    All turned with disgust from the scene.
The worms they crept in, and the worms they crept out,
And sported his eyes and his temples about,
    While the spectre addressed Imogene:

"Behold me, thou false one! behold me!" he cried;
    "Remember Alonzo the Brave!
God grants, that, to punish thy falsehood and pride,
My ghost at thy marriage should sit by thy side,
Should tax thee with perjury, claim thee as bride,
    And bear thee away to the grave!"

Thus saying, his arms round the lady he wound,
    While loudly she shrieked in dismay;
Then sank with his prey through the wide-yawning ground:
Nor ever again was Fair Imogene found,
    Or the spectre who bore her away.

Not long lived the Baron: and none since that time
    To inhabit the castle presume;
For chronicles tell, that, by order sublime,
There Imogene suffers the pain of her crime,
    And mourns her deplorable doom.

At midnight four times in each year does her sprite,
    When mortals in slumber are bound,
Arrayed in her bridal apparel of white,
Appear in the hall with the skeleton-knight,
    And shriek as he whirls her around.

While they drink out of skulls newly torn from the grave,
    Dancing round them pale spectres are seen:
Their liquor is blood, and this horrible stave
They howl: "To the health of Alonzo the Brave,
    And his consort, the False Imogene!"

<39>

Giles Jollup the Grave,
and Brown Sally Green

Original — M. G. LEWIS

*This is a parody upon the foregoing Ballad.[1] I must acknowledge,
however, that the lines printed in italics, and the idea of making an
apothecary of the knight, and a brewer of the baron, are taken from a
parody which appeared in one of the newspapers[2], under the title of
"Pil-Garlic[3] the Brave, and Brown Celestine."*

A doctor so prim and a sempstress so tight
    Hob-a-nobbed in some right marasquin[4];
They sucked up the cordial with truest delight;
Giles Jollup the Grave *was just five feet in height,*
    And four feet the brown Sally Green.

— "And as," said Giles Jollup, "to-morrow I go
    To physic a feverish land,
At some sixpenny hop, or perhaps the Mayor's show,
You'll tumble in love with some smart City beau,
    And with him share your shop in the Strand."

"Lord! how can you think so?" brown Sally Green said;
    You must know mighty little of me;
For if you be living, or if you be dead,
I swear, 'pon my honour, that none in your stead
    Shall husband of Sally Green be.

---

[1] This poem was published as a note in the fourth and fifth editions of Lewis's
novel, *The Monk*. It would seem to demonstrate that Lewis preferred being
noticed and ridiculed, to not being noticed at all, in which wisdom he
anticipates Oscar Wilde.
[2] Lewis's parody itself must have been in a newspaper, since it is reprinted in
Spirit of the Public Journals for 1799 (1:321).
[3] *Pil-garlic.* A bald man.
[4] Marasquin. A liqueur made from maraschino cherries. This line is cited in the
OED as the earliest documented print appearance of the word "marasquin."

<40>

"And if e'er for another my heart should decide,
    False to you and the faith which I gave,
God grant that, at dinner too amply supplied,
Over-eating may give me a pain in my side;
May your ghost then bring rhubarb to physic the bride,
    "And send her well-dosed to the grave!" —

Away went poor Giles, to what place is not told;
    Sally wept till she blew her nose sore!
But scarce had a twelvemonth elapsed, when behold!
A brewer, quite stylish, his gig that way roll'd,
    And stopped it at Sally Green's door.

His wealth, his pot-belly, and whisky of cane,
    Soon made her untrue to her vows:
The steam of strong beer now bewildering her brain,
He caught her while tipsy! denials were vain,
    So her carried her home as his spouse.

And now the roast beef had been blessed by the priest,
    To cram now the guests had begun:
Tooth and nail like a wolf fell the bride on the feast;
Nor yet had the clash of her knife and fork ceased,
    When a bell ('twas a dustman's) toll'd — "one!"

Then first with amazement brown Sally Green found
    That a stranger was stuck by her side:
His cravat and ruffles with snuff were embrowned;
He ate not, he drank not, but, turning him round,
    Sent some pudding away to be fried!!!

His wig was turned forwards, and short was his height:
    His apron was dirty to view:
The women (oh! wondrous) were hushed at his sight:
The cats, as they eyed him, drew back (well they might),
    For his body was pea-green and blue!

<41>

Now, as all wished to speak, but none knew what to say,
    They looked mighty foolish and queer:
At length spoke the bride, while she trembled — "I pray,
Dear sir, your peruke that aside you would lay,
    And partake of some strong or small beer!"—

The semptress is silent; the stranger complies,
    And his wig from his phiz deigns to pull.
Adzooks! what a squall Sally gave through surprize!
Like a pig that is stuck how she open'd her eyes,
    When she recognized Jollup's bare skull!

Each miss then exclaimed, while she turned up her snout,
    — "Sir, your head isn't fit to be seen!" —
The potboys ran in, and the potboys ran out,
And couldn't conceive what the noise was about,
    While the Doctor addressed Sally Green:

— "Behold me, thou jilt-flirt! behold me!" he cried;
    "You've broken the faith which you gave!
God grants, that to punish your falsehood and pride,
Over-eating should give you a pain in your side:
Come, swallow this rhubarb! I'll physic the bride,
    And send her well-dosed to the grave!"

Thus saying, the physic her throat he forced down,
    In spite of whate'er she could say;
Then bore to his chariot the damsel so brown;
Nor ever again was she seen in that town,
    Or the Doctor who whisked her away.

Not long lived the Brewer: and none since that time
    To make use of the brewhouse presume;
For 'tis firmly believed, that, by order sublime,
There Sally Green suffers the pain of her crime,
    And bawls to get out of the room.

<42>

At midnight four times in each year does her sprite
    With shrieks make the chamber resound:
"I won't take the rhubarb!" she squalls in affright;
While, a cup in his left hand, a draught in his right,
    Giles Jollup pursues her around!

With wigs so well powdered, their fees while they crave,
    Dancing round them twelve doctors are seen;
They drink chicken-broth, while this horrible stave
Is twanged through each nose: "To Giles Jollup the Grave,
    And his patient, the sick Sally Green!"

<43>

Elver's Hoh

Danish/German — M. G. LEWIS [after HERDER]

The original is to be found in the Kiampe-Viiser, Copenhagen, 1739[1]. *My version of this Ballad (as also of most of the Danish Ballads in this collection) was made from a German translation to be found in Herder's*[2] Volkslieder[3].

The knight laid his head upon Elver's Hoh,
    Soft slumbers his senses beguiling;
Fatigue pressed its seal on his eyelids, when lo!
    Two maidens drew near to him, smiling;
The one she kissed softly Sir Algamore's eyes;
    The other she whispered him sweetly,
— "Arise! thou gallant young warrior, arise,
    For the dance it goes gaily and featly!

"Arise, thou gallant young warrior, arise,
    And dance with us now and for ever!
My damsels with music thine ear shall surprise,
    And sweeter a mortal heard never."
Then straight of young maidens appeared a fair throng,
    Who their voices in harmony raising,
The winds they were still as the sounds flew along,
    By their silence their melody praising.

---

[1] *Kiampe-Viiser.* Lewis's — and Herder's — original is from the 1695 Danish compilation by Anders Sörensen Vedel and Peder Syv, *Et Hundrede udvalde Danske Viser.* An earlier collection by Vedel from 1591, and several later compilations, are referred to collectively as the *Kæmpe-Viser* (Farley 177).
[2] *Herder.* Johann Gottfried von Herder (1744-1803), German poet, critic, and philosopher. Karl Guthke remarks that Lewis was "the first to bring out translations from Herder in Herder's name" (52).
[3] *Volkslieder.* Herder's *Volkslieder*, Book 2, No. 14 (185-88).

<44>

The winds they were still as the sounds flew along,
    The wolf howl'd no more from the mountains;
The rivers were mute upon hearing the song,
    And calm'd the loud rush of their fountains;
The fish as they swam in the waters so clear,
    To the soft sounds delighted attended,
And nightingales, charm'd the sweet accents to hear,
    Their notes with the melody blended.

— "Now hear me, thou gallant young warrior, now hear!
    If thou wilt partake of our pleasure,
We'll teach thee to draw the pale moon from her sphere,
    We'll show thee the sorcerer's treasure!
We'll teach thee the Runic rhyme, teach thee to hold
    The wild bear in magical fetters,
To charm the red dragon, who broods over gold,
    And tame him by mystical letters." —

Now hither, now thither, then danced the gay band,
    By witchcraft the hero surprising,
Who ever sat silent, his sword in his hand,
    Their sports and their pleasures despising.
— "Now hear me, thou gallant young warrior, now hear!
    If still thou disdain'st what we proffer,
With dagger and knife from thy breast will we tear
    Thine heart, which refuses our offer!" —

Oh! glad was the knight when he heard the cock crow!
    His enemies trembled and left him:
Else must he have stayed upon Elver's Hoh,
    And the witches of life had bereft him.
Beware then, ye warriors, returning by night
    From Court, dressed in gold and in silver;
Beware how you slumber on Elver's rough height,
    Beware of the witches of Elver!

<45>

The Sword of Angantyr

Runic — M. G. LEWIS

*The original is to be found in Hickes[1]' Thesau. Lit. Septen[2]. I have
taken great liberties with it, and the catastrophe is my own invention.[3]
Several versions of this Poem have already appeared[4], particularly one
by Miss Seward.*— MGL

[*Bishop Percy provides the following Introduction to the poem:*
"Andgrym the grandfather of Hervor, was prince of a part of Sweden, now in
the province of Smaland: He forcibly carried away out of Russia Eyvor the
daughter of Suafurlama, by whom he had twelve sons, four whereof were
Hervardur, Hiorvardur, Hrani, and Angantyr the father of Hervor. These
twelve brethren, according to the usual practice of those times, practiced piracy.
In one of their expeditions they landed in the territories of Hialmar king of

---

[1] *Hickes*. George Hickes, D.D. (1642-1715). A theologian and polymath who,
when he was not immersed in ecclesiastic and political debates, devoted the
remainder of his time to researching the oldest documents and relics of Anglo-
Saxon history, including the Icelandic sagas. He was, in his day, regarded as one
of the most learned men in England. He had access to original Saxon manu-
scripts that are no longer extant. Hickes' work has been called "a monumental
project by Britain's first old northern philological giant" (Wawn, *Vikings*, 19).

[2] *Thesau. Lit. Septen*. Bishop Percy cites Hickes' "*Thesauarus Antiq. Literaturae
Septentrion*, Vol. 1, p. 193" as his source. Lewis cites "Thesau. Ling. Septen" and
misspells Hickes' name. Since Lewis comes far closer to the actual title of the
book, *Linguarum Veterum Septentrionalium Thesaurus Grammatico-Criticus et
Aechaeologicus*, he is unlikely to have merely cribbed the source title from Percy,
whose printer got it wrong. Margaret Clunies Ross has detailed Percy's work as
translator in a fine monograph, *The Old Norse Poetic Translations of Thomas Percy*.

[3] The ending of this version of the poem is indeed Lewis's own. The poet seems
unwilling to leave a female protagonist unravished or alive. Since the poem is an
episode in the long and violent career of the female heroine of *The Hervarer Saga*,
Lewis does considerable violence, undermining Hervor's epic, rather like having
Superman killed by a bus on his first day in Metropolis. Hervor, dressed in a
male warrior's attire, is in the grand gender-transgressive tradition of women
warriors and maiden kings. After the end of Lewis's poem, I have appended the
original ending, as translated/adapted by Percy.

[4] *Several versions*... The Runic poem was widely known, translated by Percy as
"The Incantation of Hervor" in *Five Pieces of Runic Poetry Translated from the
Icelandic Language* (1763). Lewis does not mention Herder, whose German
version of this appears in *Volkslied*, Vol. 2 No 15 as "Zauberspräch Angantyrs
und Hervors." Since it immediately follows "Elvers Hoh" in Herder's book, it is
inconceivable that Lewis did not use Herder's poem as his principal model.
Muddying our perception further, one should add that Herder is known to have
read Percy's English versions.

<46>

Thulemark, where a fierce battle ensuing they all lost their lives. Angantyr fell the last of his brethren, having first with his own hand killed their adversary Hialmar. They were buried in the field of battle, together with their arms: and it is at their tombs that Hervor, who had taken a voyage thither on purpose, makes the following invocation"[5]—BR].

HERVOR

Angantyr[6], awake! awake!
   Hervor bids thy slumbers fly!
Magic thunders round thee break,
   Angantyr, reply! reply![7]

Reach me, warrior, from thy grave
   Schwafurlama's magic blade;
Fatal weapon, dreaded glaive,[8]
   By the dwarfs[9] at midnight made.

Hervardur[10], obey my charms,
   Hanri too, and Angantyr:
Hither, clad in bloody arms,
   Haste with helmet, sword, and spear!

---

[5] Introduction from Percy, *Five Pieces of Runic Poetry* (1763, pp. 3-4).

[6] *Angantyr.* "One who bravely does his duty" (Olaus Verelius 49). Angantyr and his twelve warrior brothers were berserkers, famous for warlike exploits, but also for acts committed in uncontrollable rage.

[7] The original Icelandic has an epic, rhetorical force. The opening lines transliterate as "Vakadnu Angantyr! / Vekur thig Hervor/ Einka dotter/ Yckar Suafu:/ Sel thu mer ur hauge/ Hardan maekir,/ Than er Suafurlama/ Slogu duergar."

[8] *Glaive.* A broadsword.

[9] *Dwarfs.* Percy cites Olaus Verelius, who prepared the earliest print edition of *The Hervarer Saga* in Swedish in 1672, with the observation that the dwarfs mentioned here are not the diminutive creatures of children's fairy tales, but instead a powerful race of lesser demons whose specialty is the manufacture of weapons (*Verelius*, Vol 2: 44-45).

[10] *Hervardur.* "A preserver of the army" (Olaus Verelius 49).

<47>

Hasten, heroes, hasten all;
    Sadly pace the spell-bound sod;
Dread my anger, hear my call,
    Tremble at the charmer's rod!

Are the sons of Angrym's race[11],
    They whose breasts with glory burned,
All deprived of manhood's grace,
    All to dust and ashes turn'd?

Where the blasted yew-tree grows,
    Where the bones of heroes lie,
What, will none his grave unclose,
    None to Hervor's voice reply?

Shades of warriors cold and dead,
    Fear my wrath, nor longer stay!
Mighty souls to Hela fled,
    Come! my powerful spells obey.

Either instant to my hand
    Give the sword of mystic power,
Which the dwarf and spectre-band
    Bathed in blood at midnight hour;

Or, in Odin's hall of cheer,
    Never shall ye more repose,
Never more drink mead and beer
    From the skulls of slaughter'd foes!

ANGANTYR

Hervor! Hervor! cease thy cries,
    Nor oblige, by impious spell,
Ghosts of slaughter'd chiefs to rise;
    Sport not with the laws of hell!

---

[11] *Angrym.* Angrym or Arngrim was Angantyr's father.

<48>

Know, nor friend's, nor parent's hand
    Laid in earth's embrace my bones:
Natives of a distant land
    Raised yon monumental stones:

I the Tyrfing[12] gave to these;
    'Twas but justice; 'twas their due.
Hervor! Hervor! rest in peace,
    Angantyr has told thee true.

HERVOR

Dar'st thou still my anger brave?
    Thus deceitful dar'st thou speak?
Sure as Odin dug thy grave,
    Lies by thee the sword I seek.

I alone may call thee sire,
    I alone thine heir can be;
Give me then the sword of fire,
    Angantyr, oh! give it me!

ANGANTYR

Hervor! Hervor! cease, and know,
    It endures no female hand;
Flames around her feet shall glow,
    Who presumes to touch the brand:

But from thee a son shall spring
    (So the Valkyries[13] declare),
Who shall reign a mighty king;
    He the magic blade shall wear.

---

[12] *Tyrfing*. The name of the sword Angantyr received from his father. The blade could cut through any material, and a man died each time the sword was unsheathed.

[13] *Valkyries*. Maidens who carry the souls of slain heroes to Valhalla.

<49>

HERVOR

Hela! Hela! thrice around
    This enchanted spot I pace:
Hela! Hela! thrice the ground
    Thus with mystic signs I trace.

While I swear by Odin's might,
    Balder's[14] locks, and Sculda's wing,
By the god renowned in fight,
    By the rhymes the sisters[15] sing,

Still the dead unrest shall know,
    Still shall wave my magic rod,
Still the shivering ghosts shall go
    Round and round this spell-bound sod,

Till the sword, the death of shields,
    Shall my sire to me resign;
Till my hand the Tyrfing wields,
    As in *his* grasp, fear'd in mine!

ANGANTYR

Bold enchantress, since no prayers
    Can this impious zeal abate;
Since thy haughty bosom dares
    To dispute the will of Fate,

---

[14] *Balder*. A beloved Nordic god, son of Odin and Frigg, a kind of Nordic Achilles, who seemed indestructible, until felled and killed by a piece of mistletoe (Mallet-Percy, Vol. 2, pp. 103-105).
[15] *Sisters*. In the *Eddas*, the Valkyries have two roles: choosing who will die in battle, and then carrying the fallen to Valhalla. Alternately, the Norns, the Nordic equivalent of the Three Fates, are given the task of tending the loom that marks the hero's lifeline, and choosing when the hero will die. Lewis here treats both roles as belonging to Valkyries.

<50>

I no more retard thy doom:
    Armed with magic helm and spear
Seek the Tyrfing, seek my tomb,
    When the midnight hour is near.

HERVOR

Stormy clouds around me lour!
    All is silent, mortals sleep!
'Tis the solemn midnight hour!
    Angantyr, thy promise keep.

'Tis the time, and here the grave:
    Lo! the grate with pain I lift:
Father, reach me forth the glaive,
    Reach the dwarf's enchanted gift.

ANGANTYR

Know beneath my head it lies,
    Deep embrowned with hostile gore.
Hervor, daughter, cease thy cries,
    Hervor, daughter, ask no more.

Flames curl round in many a spire,
    Flames from Hilda's mystic hand;
Ne'er may woman touch the fire,
    Ne'er may woman wield the brand!

HERVOR

Wherefore, father, this delay,
    Wherefore break the word you gave?
Coldly burn the flames which play
    In a breathless warrior's grave.

<51>

Give me straight the spell-fraught sword,
    Then my potent charms shall cease:
Be the dead to sleep restored,
    Rest, sad spirit, rest in peace!

ANGANTYR

Oh! what demon's direful power,
    Hapless Hervor, fires thy brain?
Fain would I retard the hour,
    Destined for my daughter's pain!

Yet be wise, the sword forego:
    It endures no female hand;
Flames around her feet shall glow,
    Who presumes to touch the brand.

HERVOR

Wilt thou still the brand conceal?
    I must haste my friends to join,
Where Hidalvar, clad in steel,
    Leads his troops, and waits for mine:

Father, now the sword bestow;
    Soon 'twill hew my path to fame;
Soon 'twill make each trembling foe
    Shrink with fear at Hervor's name!

ANGANTYR

Hark! what horrid voices ring
    Through the mansions of the dead!
'Tis the Valkyries who sing,
    While they spin thy vital thread.

<52>

— "Angantyr!" I hear them say,
    Sitting by their magic loom,
— "Yield the sword, no more delay,
    Let the sorceress meet her doom!

"Soon the proud one shall perceive,
    Anguish ends what crimes begin:
Lo! her web of life we weave,
    Lo! the final thread we spin!" —

I obey the voice of hell,
    It ensures repose to me:
Hervor, now unbind the spell,
    And the Tyrfing thine shall be.

HERVOR

Since thy dread commands, my sire,
    Force the Tyrfing to forego,
On thine altars, sisters dire,
    Thrice twelve heroes' blood shall flow.

With respect the mandate hear;
    Angantyr, the sword resign:
Valued gift, to me more dear,
    Than were Norway's sceptre mine.

ANGANTYR

I obey! the magic glaive
    Thirty warriors' blood hath spilt;
Lo! I reach it from my grave,
    Death is in the sheath and hilt!

Now 'tis thine: that daring arm
    Wields at length the flaming sword;
Hervor, now unbind the charm,
    Be my ghost to sleep restored.

<53>

HERVOR

Rest in peace, lamented shade!
    Be thy slumbers soft and sweet,
While, obtained the wondrous blade,
    Home I bend my gladsome feet.

But from out the gory steel
    Streams of fire their radiance dart!
Mercy! mercy! oh! I feel
    Burning pangs invade my heart!

Flames amid my ringlets play,
    Blazing torrents dim my sight!
Fatal weapon, hence away!
    Woe be to thy blasting might!

Woe be to the night and time,
    When the magic sword was given!
Woe be to the Runic rhyme,
    Which reversed the laws of Heaven!

Curst be cruel Hilda's fire,
    Which around the weapon curled!
Curst the Tyrfing's vengeful ire,
    Curst myself, and curst the world.

What! can nothing cool my brain?
    Nothing calm my anguish wild?
Angantyr, oh, speak again!
    Father! father! aid your child!

ANGANTYR

'Tis in vain your shrieks resound,
    Hapless prey of strange despair!
'Tis in vain you beat the ground,
    While you rend your raven hair!

<54>

They, who dare the dead to wake,
 Still too late the crime deplore:
None shall now my silence break,
 Now I sleep to wake no more!

HERVOR

Curses! curses! oh! what pain!
 How my melting eye-balls glow!
Curses! curses! through each vein
 How do boiling torrents flow!

Scorching flames my heart devour!
 Nought can cool them but the grave!
Hela! I obey thy power,
 Hela! take thy willing slave!

<55>

ANGANTYR. False woman, thou dost not understand that thou speakest foolishly of that in which thou dost rejoice: for Tirfing shall, if thou doest believe me, maid, destroy all thy offspring.

HERVOR. I must go to my seamen. Here I have no mind to stay longer. Little do I care, O royal ancestor, about what my sons may hereafter quarrel.

ANGANTYR. Take and keep Hialmar's bane, which thou shalt long have and enjoy; touch but the edge of it, there is poison in them both: it is a most cruel devourer of men.

HERVOR. I shall keep, and take in hand, the sharp sword, which thou hast let me have: I do not fear, O slain father, about what my sons may hereafter quarrel.

ANGANTYR. Farewell, daughter: I do quickly give thee twelve men's death: if thou canst believe with might and courage: even all the goods, which Andgrym's sons left behind them.

HERVOR. Dwell all of you safe in the tomb. I must be gone, and hasten hence; for I seem to be in the midst of a place where fire burneth round about me.[17]

---

[16] Thomas Percy. *Five Pieces of Runic Poetry* (1763), pp. 19-20.

[17] Patricia Terry's fine 1969 translation of the poem ends simply with "Now I have walked between the worlds/ I have seen the fires circling." (252) She explains 'between the worlds' thus: "that forbidden region . . . where Hervor talks to her father in his burial mound. Angantyr's body and his spirit are intact in the grave — dissolution seems to be the fate of cowards, and Hervor in her rage wishes it on the invisible warriors — but something in the tone of his voice, weary and even, suggests an infinite distance between him and the girl. Hervor herself, once she has the sword, hurries away from the place where she has walked through the fires of illusion with which the dead frighten the living" (xiii).

<56>

King Hacho's[1] Death-Song

Runic.   M.G. LEWIS [after EYVINDUR[2]-HERDER]

The original, but in a mutilated state, is inserted in Bartholin, Caus.
Contemt. Mort.[3] Here again, as also for the translations of "The Water
King," and of the "Erl King's Daughter," I must express my obligations to
Mr. Herder's Collection—MGL.

"Hacon was son of the celebrated Harold Harfax, [the first king of all
Norway] whose death is recorded in Regner's Ode. He was the great hero
of the Norwegians, and the last of their Pagan kings. Hacon was slain
about the year 960, in a battle with the Danes, in which eight of his
brethren fell before him. Eyvindur, his cousin, a famous scald or poet, who
was present at the battle, composed this poem to be sung at his funeral. —
What seems to have suggested the plan of the ode, was Hacon's surviving
the battle, and afterwards dying of his wounds, which were not at first
apprehended to be mortal. Although this is not very clear from the history,
something of this kind must be understood, to render the poem intelligible."

— Percy

---

[1] *Hacho.* Actually Hakon the Good, King of Norway, 934-961 CE. Mallet and
Percy render the name as "Hacon" and Lewis got "Hacho" possibly as a
misreading of Herder's black-letter German script. This is "König Hako's
Todesgesang" in *Volkslieder* Vol. 2 No. 16 pp. 198-207. I have inserted Percy's
Introduction from *Five Icelandic Poems* above the poem. This poem is also known
as *The Elogium of Hacon.*

[2] A modern edition of Sturluson's *Heimskringla, or the Lives of the Norse Kings,*
names the poet as Eyvind Scaldaspiller and the poem as "Hakonarmal." A.H.
Smith's English translation is given there (99-101).

[3] Percy traced the tortuous path of this work thus: "The Icelandic original of
this poem is preserved in Snorro Sturleson's *Hist. Regum Septentrionalium*, fol.
Vol. 1 p. 163. The Latin version of Peringskiold has been chiefly followed, except
in some places, in which preference was given to that of [Thom] Bartholin, in
his *Causae de Contempt. a Danis Mortis* [Lib. 2, Cap. II] , and to the French prose
translation of the Chev. Mallet (Percy-Mallet 181-185). Lewis asserts a
familiarity with the Bartholin Latin version, but in fact uses Herder as his
model.

<57>

Gaundul and Skogul[4] came from Thor[5]
To choose a king from out the war,
Who to Valhalla's[6] joys should speed,
And drink with Odin[7] beer and mead.[8]

Of Ingwa's race the king renown'd,
Biarner's brother, soon they found,
As arm'd with helmet, sword, and shield,[9]
With eager step he sought the field,
Where clashing glaives[10] and dying cries
Already told the combat's rise.

With mighty voice he bids appear
Haleyger brave, and Halmygeer,
Then forth to urge the fight he goes,
The hope of friends, and fear of foes.
The Norman host soon round him swarms,
And Jutland's monarch stands in arms.

Firmly is grasped by Hacho bold,
The millstone-splitter's hilt of gold,
Whose blows give death on every side,
And, as 'twere water, brass divide;
A cloud of javelins veils the sky;
The crashing shields in splinters fly;

---

4 *Skogul*. Lit. "Raging." One of the Valkyrie maidens ("choosers of the slain") who transport dead heroes to Valhalla, Skogul is associated with the arrival and announcement of Kings in Valhalla. Percy calls Gondul and Skogul "the goddesses of destiny."

5 *Thor*. Norse god of thunder, lightning, and the seasons. Armed with a mace or club, he is the defender and avenger of the gods.

6 *Valhalla*. Dwelling place of dead heroes in Norse mythology.

7 *Odin*. King of the gods, Norse form of the German Wotan, "the terrible and severe god; the father of slaughter; the god that carrieth desolation are fire" (*The Eddas*, from Percy-Mallet 73).

8 *Mead*. Fermented beverage made with honey and yeast.

9 *Shield*. Scandinavian shields were narrow, and as long as the warrior's full height. For details on the versatility of the shield, even as a flotation device, see Percy-Mallet 202-205.

10 *Glaive*. Generally, a broadsword. The word can also refer to a halberd-type weapon consisting of a blade on the end of a pole. Since the word "sword" is used later in the poem, Lewis intends the former meaning here.

<58>

And on the casques of warriors brave
Resounds the stroke of many a glaive.

Now Tyr's and Bauga's[11] weapons brown
Break on the Norman[12] monarch's crown;
Now hotter, fiercer grows the fight,
Low sinks the pride of many a knight.
And, dyed in slaughter's crimson hue,
Torrents of gore their shields bedew;
From meeting weapons lightning gleams;
From gaping wounds the life-blood streams:
With falling corses[13] groans the land,
And purple waves slash Storda's sand.

The warring heroes now confound
Buckler with buckler,[14] wound with wound:
As eager as were battle sport,
Renown they seek, and death they court;
Till, never more to rise, they fall
In myriads; while, to Odin's hall,
The daemon of the tempest brings
A blood stream on his sable wings.

---

[11] *Tyr and Bauga*. Subordinate war gods.

[12] *Normans*. Scandinavian people (Norsemen) who settled in the North of France, founding a nation that would conquer England in 1066 CE, as well as kingdoms in Sicily and southern Italy. Lewis blurs history by using the name "Norman" rather than Percy's "northern warriors" or the original poem's "Northmanns." By obscuring the historical date of the poem and by using the more modern name "Norman," the reader might mistake this for a depiction of battles during the Norman invasion of England, during which period pagan Danish invaders arrived in Britain and joined in the war. This blurring Anglicizes the narrative. Hakon's death is a century before the Norman invasion of England.

[13] *Corses*. Corpses

[14] *Buckler*. A small shield, made of leather or wood, held in the fist, used offensively to strike an opponent's face or sword arm, or defensively to deflect an opponent's blade.

<59>

Apart the hostile chiefs were placed,
Broken their swords, their helms[15] unlaced;
Yet neither thought his fate would be,
The hall of Odin soon to see.

— "Great is the feast of gods to-day,"
Propped on her sword, did Gaundul say,
"Since to their table they invite
Hacho, and all his chiefs from flight!" —

The fated monarch hears too plain,
How speaks the chooser of the slain;
Too plain beholds his startled eye,
On their black coursers[16] mounted high,
The immortal maids, who near him stand,
Each propped on her resistless brand.[17]

— "Goddess of Combat!" Hacho cries,
"Thus dost thou give the battle's prize?
And do then victory's gods deny
To view my arms with friendly eye?" —
— "Chide not!" fierce Skogul thus replied,
For conquest still shall grace thy side;
Thou shalt prevail, the foe shall yield,
And thine remain the bloody field." —

She said, and urged her coal-black steed
Swift to the hall of gods to speed;
And there to Odin's heroes tell
A king drew near with them to dwell.

---

[15] *Helm.* Helmet. "Unlaced" refers to the chinstrap holding the helmet on the head.
[16] *Courser.* A knight's battle horse, bred for strength and speed.
[17] *Brand.* "Lance" in the Percy-Mallet version (183).

<60>

"Hither," thus Odin spoke, "the king
Let Hermoder and Braga[18] bring;
A monarch comes, an hero guest,
Who well deserves with me to rest."

Said Hacho, while his streaming blood
Poured down his limbs its crimson flood,
— "God Odin's eyes, my brethren bold,
Our arms with hostile glance behold!" —

The Braga spoke: — "Brave monarch, know,
Thou to Valhalla's joys shalt go,
There to drink mead in skulls of foes,
And at the feast of gods repose:
To greet thee at the magic gate,
E'en now eight hero-brothers wait,
With joyful eyes thy coming see,
And wish, thou foe of kings, for thee." —

— "Yet be my sword," the King replied,
"Once more in Norman slaughter dyed;
Let me, as heroes should, expire,
And fall in fight, as fell my sire:
So shall my glory live, and fame
Shall long remember Hacho's name." —

He ceases, and to combat flies
He fights, he conquers, and he dies;
But soon he finds what joys attend,
Who dare in fight their days to end:
Soon as he gains Valhalla's gate,
Eight heroes there to greet him wait;
The gods a friend the monarch call,
And welcome him to Odin's hall.

---

18 *Braga*. God of poetry and eloquence.

<61>

Who in Valhalla thus shall be
Loved and revered, oh! bless'd is he;
His conquest and his fame shall long
Remember'd be, and live in song.
Wolf Fenris[19] first his claim shall break,
And on mankind his fury wreak,
Ere walks a king in Hacho's trace,
Or fills so well his vacant place.

Since to the gods the king hath fled,
Heroes and valiant hosts have bled:
The bones of friends have strow'd the sand;
Usurping tyrants sway the land;
And many a tear for Hacho brave
Still falls upon his honoured grave.

---

[19] *Wolf Fenris*. Fenrir or Fenris Ulfur, son of Loke, the giant wolf destined to devour Odin at Ragnarok (The Twilight of the Gods), the foretold end of the world: a nemesis or adversary figure feared even by the gods.

<62>

The Erl-King

German.   GOETHE. Translated by M. G. LEWIS[1]

Though founded on a Danish tradition[2], this Ballad was originally written in German, and is the production of the celebrated Goethe[3], author of "Werther," &c.

Who is it that rides through the forest so fast,
While night frowns around him, while shrill roars the blast?
The father, who holds his young son in his arm,
And close in his mantle has wrapped him up warm.

---

[1] Lewis inserted this translation into the fourth edition of *The Monk* in 1798. It was originally published in *The Monthly Mirror*, October 1796.

[2] See notes for the following poem on Herder's "The Erl-King's Daughter" as inspiration for Goethe's Erl-King.

[3] This ballad by Johann Wolfgang Goethe, author of *Faust* and *The Sorrows of Young Werther*, occupies a place of pride among German ballad poems, thanks to Schubert's setting of the poem as his first published song. The song, in which one singer imitates all four voices in the poem over a terrifying piano accompaniment, struck the art of lieder-writing like a thunderbolt. This poem, and the songs and ballads embedded inside the *Faust* dramas, remain at the apex of German art song.

<63>

"Why trembles my darling? why shrinks he with fear?"
"Oh! father! my father! the Erl-King is near!
The Erl-King, with his crown and his beard long and white!"
"Oh! your eyes are deceived by the vapours of night."

"Come, baby, sweet baby,⁴ with me go away!
Fine clothes you shall wear, we will play a fine play;
Fine flowers are growing, white, scarlet, and blue,
On the banks of yon river, and all are for you."

"Oh! father! my father! and dost thou not hear,
What words the Erl-King whispers low in mine ear?"
"Now hush thee, my darling, thy terrors appease;
Thou hear'st 'mid the branches, where murmurs the breeze."

"Oh! baby, sweet baby, with me go away!
My daughter shall nurse you, so fair and so gay;
My daughter, in purple and gold who is dressed,
Shall tend you, and kiss you, and sing you to rest!"

"Oh! father! my father! and dost thou not see
The Erl-King and his daughter are waiting for me?"
"Oh! shame thee, my darling, 'tis fear makes thee blind,
Thou seest the dark willows which wave in the wind."

"I love thee! I doat on thy face so divine!
I must and will have thee, and force makes thee mine!"
"My father! my father! oh! hold me now fast;
He pulls me, he hurts, and will have me at last!"

---

⁴ *Baby, sweet baby.* Lewis's penchant for referring to all pre-adolescents as babies
is unfortunate, and makes the poem sound ludicrous to modern readers. Lewis
could have chosen rival translations, but favored his own instead. Sir Walter
Scott's translation, for example, uses "boy" and "child," employing "infant" only
in the last line.

<64>

The father he trembled, he doubled his speed;
O'er hills and through forests he spurred his black steed;
But when he arrived at his own castle door,
Life throbbed in the sweet baby's bosom no more.

SIR WALTER SCOTT'S TRANSLATION[5]

O who rides by night thro' the woodland so wild?
It is the fond father embracing his child;
And close the boy nestles within his loved arm,
To hold himself fast, and to keep himself warm.

"O father, see yonder! see yonder!" he says;
"My boy, upon what dost thou fearfully gaze?"
"O, 'tis the Erl-King with his crown and his shroud."
"No, my son, it is but a dark wreath of the cloud."

The Erl-King Speaks:
"O come and go with me, thou loveliest child;
By many a gay sport shall thy time be beguiled;
My mother keeps for thee many a fair toy,
And many a fine flower shall she pluck for my boy."

"O father, my father, and did you not hear
The Erl-King whisper so low in my ear?"
"Be still, my heart's darling — my child, be at ease;
It was but the wild blast as it sung thro' the trees."

---

[5] Scott, impatient for the appearance of his work in Lewis's anthology, produced his own small book in 1799 titled *An Apology for Tales of Terror*, in which he included this translation. Scott's book — of which only five copies survive — also includes some of Lewis's poems available to Scott, namely those that had appeared in *The Monk*. *An Apology* is the rarest of all books in the Gothic canon. The full text of Scott's *Apology* as well as exhaustive background about the correspondence between the two writers, the research of Douglass H. Thomson, can be found online at walterscott.lib.ed.ac.uk/works/poetry/apology/contents.

<65>

Erl-King:
"O wilt thou go with me, thou loveliest boy?
My daughter shall tend thee with care and with joy;
She shall bear thee so lightly thro' wet and thro' wild,
And press thee, and kiss thee, and sing to my child."

"O father, my father, and saw you not plain
The Erl-King's pale daughter glide past thro' the rain?"
"Oh yes, my loved treasure, I knew it full soon;
It was the grey willow that danced to the moon."

Erl-King:
"O come and go with me, no longer delay,
Or else, silly child, I will drag thee away."
"O father! O father! now, now, keep your hold,
The Erl-King has seized me — his grasp is so cold!"

Sore trembled the father; he spurr'd thro' the wild,
Clasping close to his bosom his shuddering child;
He reaches his dwelling in doubt and in dread,
But, clasp'd to his bosom, the infant was dead.

<66>

GOETHE'S ERLKÖNIG

Wer reitet so spät durch Nacht und Wind?
Es ist der Vater mit seinem Kind;
Er hat den Knaben wohl in dem Arm,
Er faßt ihn sicher, er hält ihn warm.

"Mein Sohn, was birgst du so bang dein Gesicht?" —
"Siehst, Vater, du den Erlkönig nicht?
Den Erlenkönig mit Kron und Schweif?" —
"Mein Sohn, es ist ein Nebelstreif."

"Du liebes Kind, komm, geh mit mir!
Gar schöne Spiele spiel' ich mit dir;
Manch' bunte Blumen sind an dem Strand,
Meine Mutter hat manch gülden Gewand."—

"Mein Vater, mein Vater, und hörest du nicht,
Was Erlenkönig mir leise verspricht?" —
"Sei ruhig, bleibe ruhig, mein Kind;
In dürren Blättern säuselt der Wind." —

<67>

"Willst, feiner Knabe, du mit mir gehen?
Meine Töchter sollen dich warten schön;
Meine Töchter führen den nächtlichen Reihn,
Und wiegen und tanzen und singen dich ein." —

"Mein Vater, mein Vater, und siehst du nicht dort
Erlkönigs Töchter am düstern Ort?" —
"Mein Sohn, mein Sohn, ich seh es genau:
Es scheinen die alten Weiden so grau. —"

"Ich liebe dich, mich reizt deine schöne Gestalt;
Und bist du nicht willig, so brauch ich Gewalt." —
"Mein Vater, mein Vater, jetzt faßt er mich an!
Erlkönig hat mir ein Leids getan!" —

Dem Vater grauset's, er reitet geschwind,
Er hält in Armen das ächzende Kind,
Erreicht den Hof mit Müh' und Not;
In seinen Armen das Kind war tot.

<68>

The Erl-King's Daughter

Danish.   M. G. LEWIS[1]

The original is in the Kiampe-Viiser.[2]

O'er the mountains, through vallies, Sir Oluf he wends
To bid to his wedding relations and friends;
'Tis night, and arriving where sports the elf band,
The Erl-King[3]'s proud daughter presents him her hand.

— "Now welcome, Sir Oluf! oh! welcome to me!
Come, enter our circle my partner to be." —
— "Fair lady, nor can I dance with you, nor may;
To-morrow I marry, to-night must away." —

— "Now listen, Sir Oluf; oh, listen to me!
Two spurs of fine silver thy guerdon shall be;
A shirt too of silk will I give as a boon,
Which my queen-mother bleached in the beams
        of the moon.

"Then yield thee, Sir Oluf! oh, yield thee to me!
And enter our circle my partner to be."
— "Fair lady, nor can I dance with you, nor may;
"To-morrow I marry, to-night must away." —

---

[1] Lewis inserted this translation into the fourth edition of *The Monk* in 1798. Originally published in *The Monthly Mirror*, October 1796.

[2] *Kiampe-Viiser.* The 1695 Danish compilation by Anders Sörensen Vedel and Peder Syv, *Et Hundrede udvalde Danske Viser.* An earlier collection by Vedel from 1591, and several later compilations, are referred to collectively as the *Kæmpe-Viser* (Farley 177). As Lewis notes earlier, he has adapted Herder's translation ("Erlkönigs Tochter," *Volkslieder*, Part 2, Book 2, 27 pp. 224-227). Goethe's famous poem, "Erlkönig," has a different story-line, but is directly inspired by Herder's poem.

[3] *Erl-King.* From the Danish *elverkonge*, or Elf-King. This makes "Erlkönig" a borrowed word in German, literally meaning "Alder-King" in that language. The Erl-King is associated with omens of death, much like the Irish banshee. This story is fairy lore, and not part of the Wotan mythos.

<69>

— "Now listen, Sir Oluf; oh, listen to me!
An helmet of gold will I give unto thee!" —
— "A helmet of gold would I willingly take,
"But I will not dance with you, for Urgela's sake." —

— "And deigns not Sir Oluf my partner to be?
Then curses and sickness I give unto thee;
Then curses and sickness thy steps shall pursue:
Now ride to thy lady, thou lover so true." —

Thus said she, and laid her charmed hand on his heart; —
Sir Oluf, he never had felt such a smart;
Swift spurred he his steed till he reached his own door,
And there stood his mother his castle before.

— "Now riddle me, Oluf, and riddle me right:
Why look'st thou, my dearest, so wan and so white?" —
— "How should I not, mother, look wan and look white?
I have seen the Erl-King's cruel daughter to-night.

"She cursed me! her hand to my bosom she pressed;
Death followed the touch, and now freezes my breast!
She cursed me, and said, 'To your lady now ride;'
Oh! ne'er shall my lips press the lips of my bride." —

— "Now riddle me, Oluf, and what shall I say,
When here comes the lady, so fair and so gay?" —
"Oh! say I am gone for awhile to the wood,
To prove if my hounds and my coursers are good." —

Scarce dead was Sir Oluf, and scarce shone the day,
When in came the lady, so fair and so gay;
And in came her father, and in came each guest,
Whom the hapless Sir Oluf had bade to the feast.

<70>

They drank the red wine, and they ate the good cheer;
— "Oh! where is Sir Oluf? oh, where is my dear?" —
— "Sir Oluf is gone for awhile to the wood,
To prove if his hounds and his coursers are good." —

Sore trembled the lady, so fair and so gay;
She eyed the red curtain; she drew it away;
But soon from her bosom for ever life fled,
For there lay Sir Oluf, cold, breathless, and dead.

<71>

The Water-King[1]

Danish — M. G. LEWIS.

The Original is in the Kiampe-Viiser.[2]

With gentle murmur flow'd the tide,
While by its fragrant flowery side
The lovely maid, with carols gay,
To Mary's church pursued her way.

The Water-Fiend's malignant eye
Along the banks beheld her hie;
Straight to his mother-witch he sped,
And thus in suppliant accents said:

— "Oh! mother! mother! now advise,
How I may yonder maid surprise:
Oh! mother! mother! now explain,
How I may yonder maid obtain." —

The witch she gave him armour white;
She formed him like a gallant knight:
Of water clear next made her hand
A steed, whose housings were of sand.

---

1 Lewis included this translation in the first edition of *The Monk* in 1796. It was
also published anonymously in *Scots Magazine,* March 1797.
2 *Kiampe-Viiser.* The 1695 Danish compilation by Anders Sörensen Vedel and
Peder Syv, *Et Hundrede udvalde Danske Viser.* An earlier collection by Vedel from
1591, and several later compilations, are referred to collectively as the *Kæmpe-
Viser* (Farley 177). Lewis has adapted Herder's translation ("Der Wassermann,"
Volkslieder, Part 2, Book 2:26, pp. 221-223). As will be seen from the literal
translation he appends, Lewis has greatly expanded upon the original, very
much in the folk-ballad tradition.

<72>

The Water-King then swift he went;
To Mary's church his steps he bent:
He bound his courser to the door,
And paced the churchyard three times four.

His courser to the door bound he,
And paced the churchyard four times three;
Then hastened up the aisle, where all
The people flocked, both great and small.

The priest said, as the knight drew near,
— "And wherefore comes the white chief here?" —
The lovely maid she smiled aside:
— "Oh! would I were the white chief's bride!" —

He stepped o'er benches one and two;
— "Oh! lovely maid, I die for you!" —
He stepped o'er benches two and three;
— "Oh! lovely maiden, go with me!" —

Then sweetly smiled the lovely maid;
And while she gave her hand, she said,
— "Betide me joy, betide me woe,
O'er hill, o'er dale, with thee I go." —

The priest their hands together joins;
They dance, while clear the moonbeam shines:
And little thinks the maiden bright,
Her partner is the Water-Spright.

Oh! had some spirit deign'd to sing,
— "Your bridegroom is the Water-King!" —
The maid had fear and hate confess'd,
And cursed the hand which then she press'd.

<73>

But nothing giving cause to think
How near she strayed to danger's brink,
Still on she went, and hand in hand
The lovers reach the yellow sand.

— "Ascend this steed with me, my dear!
We needs must cross the streamlet here:
Ride boldly in; it is not deep;
The winds are hushed, the billows sleep."

Thus spoke the Water-King. The maid
Her traitor bridegroom's wish obeyed:
And soon she saw the courser lave
Delighted in his present wave.

— "Stop! stop! my love! The waters blue
E'en now my shrinking foot bedew." —
— "Oh! lay aside your fears, sweet heart!
We now have reached the deepest part." —

"Stop! stop! my love! For now I see
The waters rise above my knee." —
— "Oh! lay aside your fears, sweet heart!
We now have reached the deepest part." —

— "Stop! stop! for God's sake, stop! for oh!
The waters o'er my bosom flow!" —
Scarce was the word pronounced, when knight
And courser vanished from her sight.

She shrieks, but shrieks in vain; for high
The wild winds rising, dull the cry;
The fiend exults; the billows dash,
And o'er their hapless victim wash.

<74>

Three times, while struggling with the stream,
The lovely maid was heard to scream;
But when the tempest's rage was o'er,
The lovely maid was seen no more.

Warned by this tale, ye damsels fair,
To whom you give your love beware!
Believe not every handsome knight,
And dance not with the Water-Spright!

*As I have taken great liberties with this Ballad, and have been much
questioned as to my share in it, I shall here subjoin a literal
translation:—MGL*

THE WATER-MAN

— "Oh! mother, give me good counsel:
How shall I obtain the lovely maid?"—

She formed for him a horse of clear water,
With a bridle and saddle of sand.

She armed him like a gallant knight,
Then rode he into Mary's churchyard.

He bound his horse to the church door,
And paced round the church three times and four.

The Waterman enter'd the church;
The people thronged about him both great and small.

The priest was then standing at the altar.
— "Who can yonder white chieftain be?" —

<75>

The lovely maiden laughed aside —
— "Oh! would the white chieftain were for me!" —

He stepp'd over one stool, and over two;
— "Oh! maiden, give me thy faith and troth!" —

He stepped over stools three and four;
— "Oh! lovely maiden, go with me!" —

The lovely maid gave him her hand.
— "There hast thou my troth; I follow thee readily."—

They went out with the wedding guests:
They danced gaily, and without thought of danger.

They danced on till they reached the strand:
And now they were alone hand in hand.

— "Lovely maiden, hold my horse:
The prettiest little vessel will I bring for you." —

And when they came to the white sand,
All the ships made to land.

And when they came to deep water,
The lovely maiden sank to the ground.

Long heard they who stood on the shore,
How the lovely maiden shriek'd among the waves.

I advise you, damsels, as earnestly as I can,
Dance not with the Water-man.

<76>

The Fire-King

Original — WALTER SCOTT

"The blessings of the evil genii, which are curses, were upon him."
—Eastern Tale

(By the translator of Goethe's "Goetz of Berlichingen." For more of this gentleman's Ballads, both original and translated, see "Glenfinlas," and the poems following it.)

Bold knights and fair dames, to my harp give an ear,
Of love, and of war, and of wonder to hear,
And you haply may sigh in the midst of your glee
At the tale of Count Albert and fair Rosalie.

O see you that castle, so strong and so high?
And see you that lady, the tear in her eye?
And see you that palmer,[1] from Palestine's land,
The shell[2] on his hat, and the staff in his hand?

— "Now, palmer, grey palmer, O tell unto me
"What news bring you home from the Holy Countrie;
And how goes the warfare by Galilee's strand,
And how fare our nobles, the flower of the land?" —

---

[1] *Palmer.* A pilgrim returning from the Holy Land carried a palm leaf, or the symbol of a palm leaf, as proof of the journey made.
[2] *Shell.* A scallop shell was associated with pilgrimages to the shrine of St. James the Greater (Santiago de Compostella) in Spain, but it later became associated with pilgrimages to the Holy Land. Pilgrims wore badges with objects or symbols indicating their status as pilgrims. Initially, the badges were worn upon returning, but later were worn when setting out. The pilgrim badge helped protect pilgrims from bandits, at least if the bandits were superstitious. Shells and other shrine symbols were often cast or stamped in metal and sold as souvenirs at shrines.

<77>

—"Oh, well goes the warfare by Galilee's wave,
For Gilead, and Nablous, and Ramah we have,
And well fare our nobles by Mount Lebanon,
For the Heathen have lost, and the Christians have won." —

A rich chain of gold 'mid her ringlets there hung;
That chain o'er the palmer's grey locks has she flung;
— "Oh! palmer, grey palmer, this chain be thy fee,
For the news thou hast brought from the East Countrie.

"And, palmer, good palmer, by Galilee's wave,
Oh, saw ye Count Albert, the gentle and brave?
When the Crescent went back, and the Red-cross rushed on,
Oh, saw ye him foremost on Mount Lebanon?"

"O lady, fair lady, the tree green it grows,
O lady, fair lady, the stream pure it flows,
Your castle stands strong, and your hopes soar on high,
But lady, fair lady, all blossoms to die.

"The green boughs they wither, the thunderbolt falls,
It leaves of your castle but levin[3]-scorched walls,
The pure stream runs muddy, the gay hope is gone,
Count Albert is taken on Mount Lebanon." —

Oh, she's ta'en a horse should be fleet at her speed,
And she's ta'en a sword should be sharp at her need,
And she has ta'en shipping for Palestine's land,
To ransom Count Albert from Soldanrie's[4] hand.

---

3 *Levin.* Lightning.
4 *Suldanrie.* Sultans.

<78>

Small thought had Count Albert on fair Rosalie,
Small thought on his faith, or his knighthood had he;
A heathenish damsel his light heart had won,
The Soldan's fair daughter of Mount Lebanon.

— "Oh! Christian, brave Christian, my love wouldst thou be?
Three things must thou do ere I hearken to thee —
Our laws and our worship on thee shalt thou take,
And this thou shalt first do for Zulema's[5] sake.

"And next in the cavern, where burns evermore
The mystical flame which the Curdmans[6] adore,
Alone and in silence three nights shalt thou wake,
And this thou shalt next do for Zuleman's sake.

"And last, thou shalt aid us with counsel and hand,
To drive the Frank robbers from Palestine's land;
For my lord and my love then Count Albert I'll take,
When all this is accomplished for Zulema's sake."

"And last, thou shalt aid us with council and hand,
To drive the Frank[7] robbers from Palestine's land;
For my lord and my love then Count Albert I'll take,
When all this is accomplish'd for Zulema's sake." —

He has thrown by his helmet and cross-handled sword,
Renouncing his knighthood, denying his Lord;
He has ta'en the green caftan,[8] and turban put on,
For the love of the maiden of fair Libanon.

[5] *Zulema*. Variant of Selima. A stock female name often used in captivity and rescue dramas and operas.
[6] *Curdman*. Probably refers to the influence of Zoroastrian fire-worship among the Kurds.
[7] *Frank*. Frankish or French.
[8] *Caftan*, or kaftan. A full-sleeved, ankle-length silk or cotton cloak, tied at the waist.

<79>

And in the dread cavern, deep, deep under ground,
Which fifty steel gates and steel portals surround,
He has watch'd until daybreak, but sight saw he none,
Save the flame burning bright on its altar of stone.

Amazed was the princess, the Soldan amazed,
Sore murmured the priests as on Albert they gazed;
They search'd all his garments, and under his weeds,
They found, and took from him his rosary beads,

Again in the cavern, deep, deep underground,
He watched the lone night, while the winds whistled round;
Far off was their murmur, it came not more nigh,
The flame burn'd unmoved, and nought else did he spy.

Loud murmur'd the priests, and amazed was the king,
While many dark spells of their witchcraft they sing;
They search'd Albert's body, and lo! on his breast
Was the sign of the Cross, by his father impress'd.

The priests they erase it with care and with pain,
And the recreant return'd to the cavern again;
But as he descended a whisper there fell! —
—It was his good angel,[9] who bade him farewell! —

High bristled his hair, his heart flutter'd and beat,
And he turn'd him five steps, half resolved to retreat;
But his heart it was hardened, his purpose was gone,
When he thought of the maiden of fair Libanon.

Scarce passed he the archway, the threshold scarce trod,
When the winds from the four points of heaven were abroad;
They made each steel portal to rattle and ring,
And, borne on the blast, came the dread Fire-King.

---

9 *Good angel.* Guardian angel or *daemon.*

<80>

Full sore rocked the cavern whene'er he drew nigh,
The fire on the altar blazed bickering and high;
In volcanic explosions the mountains proclaim
The dreadful approach of the Monarch of Flame.

Unmeasured in height, undistinguish'd in form,
His breath it was lightning, his voice it was storm,
I ween the stout heart of Count Albert was tame,
When he saw in his terrors the Monarch of Flame.

In his hand a broad faulchion[10] blue-glimmer'd through smoke,
And Mount Libanon shook as the monarch he spoke: —
— "With this brand shalt thou conquer, thus long, and no more,
Till thou bend to the Cross, and the Virgin adore." —

The cloud-shrouded arm gives the weapon — and see!
The recreant receives the charm'd gift on his knee.
The thunders growl distant, and faint gleam the fires
As, borne on his whirlwind, the phantom retires.

Count Albert has armed him the Paynim[11] among,
Though his heart it was false, yet his arm it was strong;
And the Red-cross waxed faint, and the Crescent came on,
From the day he commanded on Mount Libanon.[12]

From Libanon's forests[13] to Galilee's wave,
The sands of Samaar drank the blood of the brave,
Till the Knights of the Temple,[14] and Knight of Saint John,
With Salem's King Baldwin,[15] against him came on.

---

[10] *Faulchion*. Falchion, a broadsword curved on one edge.
[11] *Paynim*. Pagan.
[12] *Mount Libanon, i.e.,* Mount Lebanon, referring generally to the western
mountain range of Lebanon rather than a specific mountain.
[13] Beirut fell to King Baldwin's forces in 1110 CE.
[14] *Knights of the Temple*. The Templars.
[15] *King Baldwin*. King Baldwin I (1058-1118 CE), a French leader of the First
Crusade, became King of Jerusalem in 1100.

<81>

The war-cymbals clatter'd, the trumpets replied,
The lances were couch'd, and they closed on each side;
And horsemen and horses Count Albert o'erthrew,
Till he pierced the thick tumult King Baldwin unto.

Against the charmed blade which Count Albert did wield,
The fence had been vain of the King's Red-cross shield;
But a page thrust him forward the monarch before,
And cleft the proud turban the renegade wore.

So fell was the dint, that Count Albert stooped low
Before the crossed shield, to his steel saddle-bow;
And scarce had he bent to the Red-cross his head —
— *"Bonne grace, notre Dame,"* — he unwittingly said.

Sore sigh'd the charmed sword, for its virtue was o'er,
It sprung from his grasp, and was never seen more;
But true men have said, that the lightning's red wing
Did waft back the brand to the dread Fire-King.

He clench'd his set teeth, and his gauntleted hand,
He stretch'd with one buffet that page on the strand;
As back from the strippling the broken casque rolled,
You might see the blue eyes, and the ringlets of gold!

Short time had Count Albert in horror to stare
On those death-swimming eyeballs and blood-clotted hair,
For down came the Templars, like Cedron[16] in flood,
And dyed their long lances in Saracen blood.

The Saracens, Curdmans, and Ishmaelites yield
To the scallop, the saltier, and crostletted shield,
And the eagles were gorged with the infidel dead
From Bethsaida's fountains to Naphthali's head.

---

[16] *Cedron.* The Brook of Cedron, in the Holy Land, which runs though a ravine
between the Mount of Olives and the Holy City.

<82>

The battle is over on Bethsaida's plain —
Oh! who is yon Paynim lies stretch'd 'mid the slain?
And who is yon page lying cold at his knee?
Oh! who but Count Albert and fair Rosalie.

The lady was buried in Salem's[17] blessed bound,
The Count he was left to the vulture and hound;
Her soul to high mercy our Lady did bring,
His went on the blast to the dread Fire-King.

Yet many a minstrel's in harping can tell
How the Red-cross it conquered, the Crescent it fell;
And lords and gay ladies have sighed, 'mid their glee,
At the tale of Count Albert and fair Rosalie.

---

[17] *Salem's. i.e.*, Jerusalem's.

<83>

The Cloud-King

Original — M. G. LEWIS.

"Adjectives have but three degrees of comparison, the positive, comparative, and superlative." — *English Grammar*.[1]

Why how now, Sir Pilgrim?[2] why shake you with dread?
    Why brave you the winds of night, cutting and cold?
Full warm was your chamber, full soft was your bed,
    And scarce by the castle-bell twelve has been tolled.

— "Oh! hear you not, Warder,[3] with anxious dismay,
    How rages the tempest, how patters the rain?
While loud howls the whirlwind, and threatens, ere day,
    To strew these old turrets in heaps on the plain!" —

Now calm thee, Sir Pilgrim! thy fears to remove,
    Know, yearly, this morning is destined to bring
Such storms, which declare that resentment and love
    Still gnaw the proud heart of the cruel Cloud-King.

---

[1] *English Grammar*. Lewis's "quote" may be just his own wording of the general rule; I was not able to find the "but three degrees" qualifier in the grammars titled "English Grammar" by Charles Butler (1634), Ben Jonson (1640) or Robert Lowth (1762), nor in the grammar section of Samuel Johnson's Dictionary (1766). American Quaker Tory grammarian Lindley Murray (1745-1826) fled to England after the American Revolution and published one of the best-selling books of his era: *English Grammar Adapted to the Different Classes of Learners* (1797). If Lewis is alluding to Murray, his closest contemporary, he has taken a poetic liberty with that author who wrote, "There are commonly reckoned three degrees of comparison: the POSITIVE, the COMPARATIVE, and the SUPERLATIVE."

[2] *Pilgrim*. In medieval times, the term Pilgrim referred to those who had made a journey to the Holy Land, either in a Crusade, or on a religious pilgrimage. Later, the term was more loosely applied to anyone presently on a journey to a holy shrine, even a local one.

[3] *Warder*. A guard.

<84>

One morning, as borne on the wings of the blast,
　　The fiend over Denmark directed his flight,
A glance upon Rosenhall's[4] turrets he cast,
　　And gazed on its lady with wanton delight:

Yet proud was her eye, and her cheek flush'd with rage,
　　Her lips with disdain and reproaches were fraught;
And lo! at her feet knelt a lovely young page,
　　And thus in soft accents compassion besought:

— "Oh! drive not, dear beauty, a wretch to despair,
　　Whose fault is so venial, a fault if it be;
For who could have eyes, and not see thou art fair?
　　Or who have a heart, and not give it to thee?

"I own I adore you! I own you have been
　　Long the dream of my night, long the thought of my day;
But no hope had my heart that its idolized queen
　　Would ever with passion *my* passion repay.

"When insects delight in the blaze of the sun,
　　They harbour no wish in his glory to share:
When kneels at the cross of her Saviour the nun,
　　He scorns not the praises she breathes in her prayer.

"When the pilgrim repairs to St. Hermegild's[5] shrine,
　　And claims of her relics a kiss as his fee,
His passion is humble, is pure, is divine,
　　And such is the passion I cherish for thee!"

---

[4] *Rosenhall.* There is no Rosenhall in Denmark, but there is Rosenholm Castle, built in 1559-1607, home of the Rosenkrantz family. The family name is used in Shakespeare's *Hamlet.*

[5] *Hermegild* is a martyr rather than a saint. Her story is told in "The Man of Law's Prologue and Tale" in Chaucer's *Canterbury Tales.*

<85>

"Rash youth! how presumest thou with insolent love,"
    Thus answered the lady, "her ears to profane,
Whom the monarchs of Norway and Jutland, to move
    Their passion to pity attempted in vain?

"Fly, fly, from my sight, to some far distant land!
    That wretch must not breathe, where Romilda⁶ resides,
Whose lips, while she slept, stole a kiss from that hand
    No mortal is worthy to press as a bride's.

"Nor e'er will I wed till some prince of the air,
    His heart at the throne of my beauty shall lay,
And the two first commands which I give him, shall swear
    (Though hard should the task be enjoined) to obey." —

She said. — Straight the castle of Rosenhall rocks
    With an earthquake, and thunders announce the Cloud-King.
A crown of red lightnings confined his fair locks,
    And high o'er each arm waved a huge sable wing.

His sandals were meteors; his blue eyes revealed
    The firmament's lustre, and light scattered round;
While his robe, a bright tissue of rain-drops congealed,
    Reflected the lightnings his temples that bound.

"Romilda!" he thundered, "thy charms and thy pride
    Have drawn down a spirit; thy fears now dismiss,
For no mortal shall call thee, proud beauty, his bride;
    The Cloud-Monarch comes to demand thee for his.

---

⁶ *Rom[h]ilda*. Norse name meaning "glorious maiden of battle." Romilda is also
a character in Handel's 1738 opera *Serse (Xerxes)*, from a 1654 libretto by Nicolò
Minato.

<86>

"My eyes furnish lightnings, my wings cloud the air,
  My hand guides the thunder, my breath wakes the storm;
And the two first commands[7] which you give me, I swear
  (Though hard should the task be enjoined) to perform." —

He said, and he seized her; then urging his flight,
  Swift bore her away, while she struggled in vain;
Yet long in her ears rang the shrieks of affright,
  Which pour'd for her danger the page Amorayn.[8]

At the Palace of Clouds soon Romilda arrived,
  When the Fiend, with a smile which her terrors increased,
Exclaimed — "I must warn my three brothers I'm wived,
  And bid them prepare for my wedding the feast." —

Than lightning then swifter thrice round did he turn,
  Thrice bitterly cursed he the parent of good,
And next in a chafing-dish hasten'd to burn
  Three locks of his hair, and three drops of his blood:

And quickly Romilda, with anxious affright,
  Heard the tramp of a steed, and beheld at the gate
A youth in white arms — 'twas the false Water-Spright,
  And behind him his mother, the sorceress, sate.

The youth he was comely, and fair to behold,
  The hag was the foulest eye ever survey'd;
Each placed on the table a goblet of gold,
  While thus to Romilda the Water-King said: —

---

[7] *Commands.* The god's vow to give his beloved anything she wishes for, with dire consequences ensuing, directly parallels the story of Zeus and Semele in Ovid's *Metamorphoses*. The "Cloud-King" is a direct stand-in for Zeus, the god of thunderstorms.

[8] *Amorayn.* This fanciful name, derived from "Amor," belittles Romilda's mortal admirer, as does his status as page (a knight's apprentice).

<87>

"Hail, Queen of the Clouds! lo! we bring thee for drink
    The blood of a damsel, both lovely and rich,
Whom I tempted, and left 'midst the billows to sink,
    Where she died by the hands of my mother, the witch.

"But seest thou yon chariot, which speeds from afar?
    The Erl-King with his daughter it brings, while a throng
Of wood-fiends and succubi sports round the car,
    And goads on the nightmares that whirl it along." —

The maid, while her eyes tears of agony pour'd,
    Beheld the Erl-King and his daughter draw near:
A charger of silver each placed on the board,
    While the fiend of the forests thus greeted her ear:

"With the heart of a warrior, Cloud Queen, for thy food,
    The head of a child on thy table we place:
She spell-struck the knight as he stray'd through the wood;
    I strangled the child in his father's embrace."[9]

The roof now divided. — By fogs half concealed,
    Suck'd from marshes, infecting the air as he came,
And blasting the verdure of forest and field,
    On a dragon descended the Giant of Flame.

Fire seemed from his eyes and his nostrils to pour;
    His breath was a volume of sulphurous smoke;
He brandished a sabre still dropping with gore,
    And his voice shook the palace when silence he broke.

— "Feast, Queen of the Clouds! the repast do not scorn;
    Feast, Queen of the Clouds! I perceive thou hast food;
To-morrow I feast in my turn, for at morn
    Shall I feed on thy flesh, shall I drink of thy blood!

---

[9] *In his father's embrace*. A direct reference to the events in Goethe's "Erl-King."

<88>

"Lo! I bring for a present this magical brand,
   The bowels of Christians have dyed it with red;
This once flamed in Albert the renegade's[10] hand,
   And is destined to-morrow to strike off thy head." —

Then paler than marble Romilda she grew,
   While tears of regret blamed her folly and pride.
"Oh! tell me, Cloud-King, if the giant said true,
   And wilt thou not save from his sabre thy bride?" —

—" 'Tis in vain, my fair lady, those hands that you wring,
   The bond is completed, the die it is cast;
For she who at night weds an element-king,
   Next morning must serve for his brother's repast." —

— "Yet save me, Cloud-King! by that love you profess'd
   Bear me back to the place whence you tore me away." —
—"Fair lady! yon fiends, should I grant your request,
   Instead of to-morrow, would eat you to-day." —

"Yet mark me, Cloud-King, spread in vain is your share,
   For my bond must be void, and escaped is your prey,
The two first commands which I give you, howe'er
   The task should be wondrous, unless you obey." —

— "Well sayst thou, Romilda; thy will, then, impart,
   But hope not to vanquish the King of the Storm,
Or baffle his skill by invention or art;
   Thou canst not command what *I* cannot perform!" —

---

[10] *Albert the Renegade.* An Albert who might be regarded with some distaste by Danes is Albert of Sweden (1338-1412). Albert seized the Swedish throne by force in 1364. Denmark sided with the deposed King Magnus Eriksson and sent troops into the eight-year civil war that roiled Sweden. After being driven out of Norway, Albert, with help from the Teutonic Knights, took possession of the Danish Gotland province.

<89>

Then clasping her hands, to the Virgin she pray'd,
  While in curses the wicked ones vented their rage.
— "Now show me the truest of lovers!" — she said,
  And lo! by her side stood the lovely young Page.

His mind was all wonder, her heart all alarms;
  She sank on his breast as he sank at her knee.
— "The truest of lovers I fold in my arms,
  Than the *truest,* now show me a *truer!*" — said she.

Then loud yell'd the demons! the cloud-fashioned halls
  Dissolved, thunder bellow'd, and heavy rains beat;
Again stood the Fair midst her own castle walls,
  And still knelt the lovely young page at her feet.

And soon for her own, and for Rosenhall's lord,
  Did Romilda the *truest of lovers* declare,
Nor e'er on his bosom one sigh could afford,
  That for him she had quitted the Monarch of Air.

Full long yonder chapel has sheltered their urns,
  Long ceased has the tear on their ashes to fall;
Yet still, when October the twentieth[11] returns,
  Roars the fiend round these turrets, and shakes Rosenhall.

---

11 *October 20.* There is some pagan poetic justice in the choice of this date, the Feast Day of St. Artemius Megalomartyr (d. 363 CE). Artemius was a general under Constantine the Great who became an Arian heretic, persecuting orthodox monks and nuns. When he reverted back to orthodoxy, he became a persecutor of pagans. In Alexandria, Egypt, he was especially cruel to pagans, destroying idols and pillaging the Temple of Serapis. He was captured, tortured and martyred in Antioch. There is a somewhat delicious irony in having elemental gods reassert their primacy annually on Artemius' day.

<90>

Oh! Pilgrim, thy fears let these annals remove,
    For day to the skies will tranquility bring;
This storm but declares that resentment and love
    Still gnaw the proud heart of the cruel Cloud-King.*

*Lest my readers should mistake the drift of the foregoing tale, and suppose its moral to rest upon the danger in which Romilda was involved by her insolence and presumption, I think it necessary to explain, that my object in writing this story was to shew young ladies that it might possibly, now and then, be of use to understand a little grammar; and it must be clear to every one, that my heroine would infallibly have been devoured by the demons, if she had not luckily understood the difference between the comparative and superlative degrees. — MGL

<91>

The fisherman

German — M. G. LEWIS.

From the German of Goethe.[1]

The water rush'd, the water swell'd,
    A fisherman sat nigh;
Calm was his heart, and he beheld
    His line with watchful eye:

While thus he sits with tranquil look,
    In twain the water flows;
Then, crowned with reeds from out the brook,
    A lovely woman rose.

To him she sung, to him she said,
    — "Why temp'st thou from the flood,
By cruel arts of man betray'd,
    Fair youth, my scaly brood?

---

[1] The Goethe ballad, "Der Fischer," was written in 1779. Goethe, in his journal, *Über Kunst und Altertum* (Vol 3, 1821), seemed to distance himself from the supernatural content, stating that his poem meant to express "the feel of the waters, the mysterious grace that lures us in to bathe in the summer." It is not uncommon for older artists to prefer talking about effect and technique, rather than about overt content. Similar stories of water sprites luring men to their deaths abound in German literature, and the tradition goes back to the legend of the Argonaut Hylas, beloved of Heracles, who was drowned by water nymphs (related in Ovid's *Metamorphoses* and other sources). An adaptation of the poem into French by Albert Du Boys, "Le Pêcheur," is the first part of Hector Berlioz' extravagant 1832 sequel to his *Symphonie Fantastique*, titled *Lelio, ou Le Retour à la Vie*. The poem was also represented in a fine 1857 painting by Frederic Leighton, *The Fisherman and the Siren*.

<92>

Frederick Leighton, *The Fisherman and the Siren* (1857).

"Ah! knew'st thou how we find it sweet
    Beneath the waves to go,
Thyself would leave the hook's deceit,
    And live with us below.

"Love not their splendour in the main
    The sun and moon to lave?
Look not their beams as bright again,
    Reflected on the wave?

"Tempts not this river's glassy blue,
    So crystal, clear and bright?
Tempts not thy shade, which bathes in dew,
    And shares our cool delight?" —

The water rush'd, the water swelled,
    The fisherman sat nigh;
With wishful glance the flood beheld,
    And long'd the wave to try.

To him she said, to him she sung,
    The river's guileful queen:
Half in he fell, half in he sprung,
    And never more was seen.

<94>

DER FISCHER

Das Wasser rauscht', das Wasser schwoll,
Ein Fischer saß daran,
Sah nach dem Angel ruhevoll,
Kühl bis ans Herz hinan.

Und wie er sitzt und wie er lauscht,
Teilt sich die Flut empor:
Aus dem bewegten Wasser rauscht
Ein feuchtes Weib hervor.

Sie sang zu ihm, sie sprach zu ihm:
"Was lockst du meine Brut
Mit Menschenwitz und Menschenlist
Hinauf in Todesglut?

Ach wüßtest du, wie's Fischlein ist
So wohlig auf dem Grund,
Du stiegst herunter, wie du bist,
Und würdest erst gesund.

Labt sich die liebe Sonne nicht,
Der Mond sich nicht im Meer?
Kehrt wellenatmend ihr Gesicht
Nicht doppelt schöner her?

Lockt dich der tiefe Himmel nicht,
Das feuchtverklärte Blau?
Lockt dich dein eigen Angesicht
Nicht her in ew'gen Tau?"

Das Wasser rauscht', das Wasser schwoll,
Netzt' ihm den nackten Fuß;
Sein Herz wuchs ihm so sehnsuchtsvoll
Wie bei der Liebsten Gruß.

Sie sprach zu ihm, sie sang zu ihm;
Da war's um ihn geschehn;
Halb zog sie ihn, halb sank er hin
Und ward nicht mehr gesehn.

<95>

The Sailor's Tale

Original — M. G. LEWIS

Landlord, another bowl of punch, and, comrades, fill your glasses!
First in another bumper toast our pretty absent lasses,
Then hear how sad and strange a sight my chance it was to see,
While lately, in the *Lovely Nan*, returning from Goree![1]

As all alone at dead of night along the deck I wander'd,
And now I whistled, now on home and Polly Parsons ponder'd,
Sudden a ghastly form appeared, in dripping trowsers rigg'd,
And soon, with strange surprise and fear, Jack Tackle's
            ghost I twigg'd.

— "Dear Tom," quoth he, "I hither come a doleful tale to tell ye!
A monstrous fish has safely stowed your comrade in his belly;
Groggy last night, my luck was such, that overboard I slid,
When a shark snapped and chewed me, just as now you
            chew that quid.

"Old Nick,[2] who seemed confounded glad to catch my soul
            a-napping,
Straight taxed me with that buxom dame, the tailor's wife
            at Wapping;[3]
In vain I begged, and swore, and jaw'd; Nick no excuse
            would hear;
Quoth he, 'You lubber, make your will, and dam'me,
            downwards steer.' —

---

[1] Gorée, first settled by the Portuguese, is a tiny island, part of the city of Dakar, off the Cape Verde peninsula in Senegal. It was a central part of the infamous Triangle Trade. The "House of Slaves" there was used to hold and transfer human cargo. As the inheritor of a Caribbean plantation, Lewis knew well the signfiicance of this place name. "Returning from Gorée" almost certainly refers to a journey on a ship bringing slaves to the New World.
[2] *Old Nick*. Familiar name for the Devil.
[3] *Wapping*. A waterfront neighborhood in London associated with sailors, also the site of an "Execution Dock" where pirates were hanged.

<96>

"Tom, to the 'foresaid tailor's wife I leave my worldly riches,
But keep yourself, my faithful friend, my brand-new
      linen breeches;
Then, when you wear them, sometimes give one thought
      to Jack that's dead,
Nor leave those galligaskins[4] off while there remains
      one thread."

At hearing Jack's sad tale, my heart, you well may think,
      was bleeding;
The spirit well perceived my grief, and seemed
      to be proceeding,
But here, it so fell out, he sneezed: — Says I, —
      "God bless you, Jack!"
And poor Jack Tackle's grimly ghost was vanished in a crack!

Now, comrades, timely warning take, and landlord fill the bowl;
Jack Tackle, for the tailor's wife, has damned his precious soul;
Old Nick's a devilish dab,[5] it seems, at snapping up a sailor's,
So if you kiss your neighbour's wife, be sure she's not a tailor's.

---

4 *Galligaskins*, also called slops. Men's breeches that reached to just below the
knees. To cover the legs completely required a second pair of *stockings*.
5 *Dab*. Expert.

<97>

The Princess and the Slave

Original — M. G. LEWIS

Where fragrant breezes sigh'd through orange bowers,
And springing fountains cool'd the air with showers,
From pomp retired, and noontide's burning ray,
The fair, the royal Nouronihar[1] lay.
The cups of roses, newly cropp'd, were spread
Her lovely limbs beneath, and o'er her head
Imprisoned nightingales attuned their throats,
And lulled the princess with melodious notes.
Here rolled a lucid stream its gentle wave
With scarce-heard murmur; while a Georgian[2] slave
Placed near the couch with feathers in her hand,
The lady's panting breast in silence fanned,
And chased the insects, who presumed to seek
Their banquet on the beauty's glowing cheek.
This slave, a mild and simple maid was she,
Of common form, and born of low degree,
Whose only charms were smiles, devoid of art,
Whose only wealth, a gentle feeling heart.

While thus within her secret loved retreat,
Half sleeping, half awake, oppress'd with heat,
The princess slumbered; near her, shrill, yet faint,
Rose the sad tones of suppliant sorrow's plaint.
She starts, and angry gazes round: when lo!
A wretched female, bent with age and woe,
Drags her unsteady feet the arbour nigh,
While every step is numbered by a sigh.

---

[1] *Nouronihar.* In William Thomas Beckford's Islamic-Gothic novel, *Vathek* (1782), Princess Nouronihar is Vathek's wife, who accompanies him on a long journey through decadence to eternal damnation. Vathek and Nouronihar are exemplars of the unbridled pursuit of forbidden knowledge and pleasure.
[2] *Georgian.* The Black Sea kingdom of Georgia was ruled by Persia and Turkey during the Middle Ages. Georgians were Christians and the Islamic invasions after 1300 demolished a highly literate culture that was well into its own Renaissance. Georgians were held as slaves throughout the latter Turkish empire.

<98>

Meagre and wan her form, her cheek is pale;
Her tattered garments scarce her limbs can veil;
Yet still, through want and grief, her air betrays
Grandeur's remains, and gleams of better days.
Soon as to Nouronihar's couch she came,
Low on the ground her weak and trembling frame
Exhausted sank; and then, with gasping breast,
She thus in plaintive tones the fair address'd:

— "If e'er compassion's tear your cheek could stain,
If e'er you languished in disease and pain,
If e'er you sympathized with age's groan,
Hear, noble lady, hear a suppliant's moan!
Broken by days of want, and nights of tears,
By sickness wasted, and oppressed by years,
Beneath our sacred Mithra's[3] scorching fire
I sink enfeebled, and with thirst expire.
Yon stream is near" oh! list a sufferer's cry,
And reach one draught of water, lest I die!" —

— "What means this bold intrusion?" cried the fair,
With peevish tone, and discontented air;
"What daring voice, with wearying plaint, infests
The sacred grove where Persia's princess rests?
Beggar begone, and let these clamours cease!
This buys at once your absence, and my peace." —

---

[3] *Mithra*. A pagan god of Indo-Iranian origin, whose worship spread into the
Roman empire and became a rival for early Christianity. Mithra's birthday,
December 25, was co-opted by the Christian church in a concerted effort to
overlay pagan holidays with their own. In referring to Mithra's "scorching fire"
Lewis mistakes Mithra for a sun-god. Mithra represents Air and Light, opposes
the forces of darkness and evil, and although the heat associated with Light
promotes life, Mithra is not properly a sun god.

<99>

Thus said the princess, and indignant frown'd,
Then cast her precious bracelet on the ground,
And turn'd again to sleep. With joyless eye
The fainting stranger saw the jewel lie:
When lo! kind Selima[4] (the Georgian's name),
Softly with water from the fountain came;
And while, with gentle grace, she gave the bowl,
Thus sweetly sad her feeling accents stole.

— "Humble and poor, I nothing can bestow,
Except these tears of pity for your woe:
'Tis all I have; but yet that all receive
From one who fain your sorrows would relieve,
From one who weeps to view such mournful scenes,
And would give more, but that her hand lacks means.
Drink, mother! drink! the wave is cool and clear,
But drink in silence, lest the princess hear!"

Scarce are these words pronounced, when, bless'd surprise!
The stranger's age-bowed figure swells its size!
No more the stamp of years deforms her face;
Her tatter'd shreds to sparkling robes give place;
Her breath perfumes the air with odours sweet;
Fresh roses spring wherever tread her feet,
And from her eyes, where reign delight and love,
Unusual splendour glitters through the grove!
Her silver wand, her form of heavenly mould,
Her white and shining robes, her wings of gold,
Her port majestic, and superior height,
Announce a daughter of the world of light!

---

[4] *Selima. Selim* means "peace" in Turkish. Selima is a feminine dimunituve.
Lewis either did not know any Georgian names, or wanted to convey that the
slave had already been a captive of Turks in that part of Georgia under their
control. Selim and Selima are common names found in captivity and rescue
dramas and operas.

<100>

The princess, whom her slave's delighted cries
Compelled once more to ope her sleep-bound eyes,
With wonder mixed with awe the scene survey'd,
While thus the Peri[5] cheer'd the captive maid:

— "Look up, sweet girl, and cast all fears aside!
I seek my darling son's predestined bride,
And here I find her: here are found alone,
Feelings as kind, as gracious as his own.
For you, fair princess, in whose eyes of blue,
The strife of envy, shame, and grief, I view,
Observe, and profit by this scene! you gave,
But oh! how far less nobly than your slave!
Your bitter speech, proud glance, and peevish tone,
Too plain declared, your gift was meant alone
Your own repose and silence to secure,
And hush the beggar, not relieve the poor!
Oh! royal lady, let this lesson prove,
Smiles, more than presents, win a suppliant's love;
And when your mandates rule some distant land,
Where all expect their blessings from your hand,
Remember, with ill-will and frowns bestow'd,
Favours offend, and gifts become a load!" —

She ceased, and touching with her silver wand
Her destined daughter, straight two wings expand
Their purple plumes, and wave o'er either arm;
Next to her person spreads the powerful charm;
And soon the enraptured wondering maid combined
A faultless person with a faultless mind.
Then, while with joy divine their hearts beat high,
Swift as the lightning of a jealous eye
The Peris spread their wings and soar'd away
To the bless'd regions of eternal day.

---

[5] *Peri*. Persian fairies or fallen angels. Beings halfway between angels and demons, believed to be exiled from Heaven for refusing to take sides in the battle between Good and Evil. Peris often visited mortals, usually doing good but also capable of great mischief. Peris themselves were often pursued and tormented by demons.

<101>

Stung with regret, the princess saw too plain,
Lost by her fault what tears could ne'er regain!
Long on the tablets of her humbled breast
The Peri's parting words remained impress'd.
E'en when her hand Golconda's[6] sceptre sway'd,
And subject realms her mild behests obey'd,
The just reproof her conscious ear still heard;
Still she remembered, with ill grace conferr'd,
Crowns, to a feeling mind, less joy impart,
Than trifles, offer'd with a willing heart.

---

[6] *Golconda*, a kingdom in southern India (Hyderabad), famed for its diamond mines. The Qutub Shai rulers of the 16th century had strong ties to Persian culture and might have intermarried with the Persian elite.

<102>

The Gay Gold Ring

Original — M. G. LEWIS

— "There is a thing, there is a thing,
Which I fain would have from thee!
I fain would have thy gay gold ring;
O! warrior, give it me!" —

He lifts his head;
Lo! near his bed
Stands a maid as fair as day;
Cold is the night,
Yet her garment is light,
For her shift is her only array.

— "Come you from east,
Or come your from west,
Or dost from the Saracens flee?
Cold is the night,
And your garment is light,
Come, sweetheart, and warm you by me!" —

— "My garment is light,
And cold is the night,
And I would that my limbs were as cold:
Groan must I ever,
Sleep can I never,
Knight, till you give me your gay ring of gold!

For that is a thing, a thing, a thing,
Which I fain would have from thee!
I fain would have thy gay gold ring;
O! warrior, give it me!" —

<103>

— "That ring Lord Brooke
From his daughter took;
He gave it to me, and he swore,
That fair la-dye
My bride would be,
When this crusade were o'er.

Ne'er did mine eyes that lady view,
Bright Emmeline by name:
But if fame say true,
Search Britain through,
You'll find no fairer dame.

But though she be fair,
She cannot compare,
I wot, sweet lass, with thee;
Then pass by my side
Three nights as my bride,
And thy guerdon the ring shall be!" —

In silence the maid
The knight obeyed;
Low on his pillow her head she laid:
But soon as by hers *his* hand was press'd,
Changed to ice was the heart in his breast;
And his limbs were fettered in frozen chains,
And turned to snow was the blood in his veins.

The cock now crows!
The damsel goes
Forth from the tent; and the blood which she froze,
Again through the veins of Lord Elmerick flows,
And again his heart with passion glows.

<104>

Donned the knight
His armour bright;
Full wroth was he, I trow!
— "Beshrew me!" he said,
"If thus, fair maid,
"From my tent to-morrow you go!" —

Gone was light!
Come was night!
The sand-glass told, 'twas three;
And again stood there
The stranger fair,
And murmur again did she.

— "There is a thing, there is a thing,
Which I fain would have from thee!
I fain would have thy gay gold ring;
O! warrior, give it me!" —

"One night by my side
Hast thou passed as my bride:
Two yet remain behind:
Three must be passed,
Ere thy finger fast
The gay gold ring shall bind." —

Again the maid
The knight obeyed;
Again on his pillow her head she laid;
And again, when by hers *his* hand was press'd,
Changed to ice was the heart in his breast:
And his limbs were fetter'd in frozen chains,
And turned to snow was the blood in his veins!

<105>

Three days were gone, two nights were spent;
Still came the maid, when the glass told "three;"
How she came, or whither she went,
None could say, and none could see;
But the warrior heard,
When night the third
Was gone, thus claimed his plighted word:

— "Once! — twice! — thrice by your side
Have I lain as your bride;
Sir Knight! Sir Knight, beware you!
Your ring I crave!
Your ring I'll have,
Or limb from limb I'll tear you!" —

She drew from his hand the ring so gay;
No limb could he move, and no word could he say.
— "See, Arthur, I bring
To my grave, thy ring," —
Murmured the maiden, and hied her away.

Then sprang so light
From his couch the knight;
With shame his cheek was red:
And, filled with rage,
His little foot-page
He called from beneath the bed.

— "Come hither, come hither,
My lad so lither;[1]
While under my bed you lay,
What did you see,
And what maiden was she,
Who left me at breaking of day?" —

---

[1] *lither*. Worthless or lazy.

<106>

— "Oh! master, I
No maid could spy,
As I've a soul to save;
But when the cock crew,
The lamp burned blue,
And the tent smell'd like a grave!

And I heard a voice in anguish moan,
And a bell seem'd four to tell;
And the voice was like a dying groan,
And the bell like a passing bell!" —

★ ★ ★

Lord Brooke look'd up, Lord Brooke look'd down,
   Lord Brooke look'd over the plain;
He saw come riding tow'rds the town,
   Of knights a jolly train:

— "Is it the king of Scottish land,
   Or the prince of some far coun-trie,
That hither leads yon goodly band
   To feast awhile with me?" —

— "Oh, it's not the prince of some far coun-trie,
   Nor the king of Scottish land:
It's Elmerick come from beyond the sea,
   To claim Lady Emmeline's hand."

Then down Lord Brooke's grey beard was seen
   A stream of tears to pour;
— "Oh! dead my daughter's spouse has been
   These seven long years and more!

"Remorseful guilt and self-despite
   Destroyed that beauteous flower,
For that her falsehood kill'd a knight;
   'Twas Arthur of the Bower.

<107>

Sir Arthur gave her his heart to have,
    And he gave her his troth to hold;
And he gave her his ring so fair and brave,
    Was all of the good red gold:

And she gave him her word, that only he
    Should kiss her as a bride;
And she gave him her oath, that ring should be
    On her hand the day she died.

But when she heard of Lord Elmerick's fame,
    His wealth, and princely state;
And when she heard, that Lord Elmericks's name
    Was praised by low and great;

Did vanity full lightly bring
    My child to break her oath,
And to you she sent Sir Arthur's ring,
    And to him sent back his troth.

Oh! when he heard,
That her plighted word
His false love meant to break,
The youth grew sad,
And the youth grew mad,
And his sword he sprang to take:

He set the point against his side,
    The hilt against the floor;
I wot he made a wound so wide,
    He never a word spake more.

And now, too late, my child began
    Remorseful tears to shed;
Her heart grew faint, her cheek grew wan,
    And she sicken'd, and took to her bed.

<108>

The Leech then said,
And shook his head,
She ne'er could health recover;
Yet long in pain
Did the wretch remain,
Sorrowing for her lover.

And sure 'twas a piteous sight to see,
   How she prayed to die, but it might not be;
And when the morning bell told three,
   Still in hollow voice cried she:

— 'There is a thing, there is a thing,
   Which I fain would have from thee!
I fain would have thy gay gold ring;
   O! warrior, give it me!' —"

★ ★ ★

Now who than ice was colder then,
   And who more pale than snow?
And who was the saddest of all sad men?
   Lord Elmerick, I trow!

— "Oh! lead me, lead me to the place
   Where Emmeline's tomb doth stand,
For I must look on that lady's face,
   And touch that lady's hand!" —

Then all who heard him, stood aghast,
   But not a word was said,
While through the chapel's yard they passed,
   And up the chancel sped.

They burst the tomb, so fair and sheen,
   Where Emmeline's corse inclosed had been;
And lo! on the skeleton's finger so lean,
   Lord Elmerick's gay gold ring was seen!

<109>

Damsels! damsels! mark aright
   The doleful tale I sing!
Keep your vows, and heed your plight,
And go to no warrior's tent by night,
   To ask for a gay gold ring.*

* I once read in some Grecian author,[2] whose name I have forgotten, the story which suggested to me the outline of the foregoing ballad. It was as follows: A young man arriving at the house of a friend, to whose daughter he was betrothed, was informed that some weeks had passed since death had deprived him of his intended bride. Never having seen her, he soon reconciled himself to her loss, especially as, during his stay at his friend's house, a young lady who was kind enough to visit him every night in his chamber, whence she retired at daybreak, always carrying with her some valuable present from her lover. This intercourse continued till accident showed the young man the picture of his deceased bride, and he recognized, with horror, the features of his nocturnal visitor. The young lady's tomb being opened, he found in it the various presents which his liberality had bestowed on his unknown *inamorata* — MGL.

---

[2] Lewis has strayed far from the familiar Greek classics here. What seems to be the parent of this story was related by the Greek philosopher Proclus (412-484 CE) in one of his treatises regarding Plato's *Republic*. Proclus cites letters written by Hipparchus and Arrhidaeus from the third century BCE as his sources, thus recounting a story already some 700 years old. Theologian Alexander Morus (1616-1670) rescued the unpublished tale from a manuscript in the Vatican. The ghost story is related in full in Lacy Collison-Morley's *Greek and Roman Ghost Stories* (1912, pp. 66-70). Lewis has altered the domestic circumstances of the story considerably, but the details and incidents are much alike. This tale is a ghost story but also a precursor of the vampire tale. Goethe adapted the same material, moving it to Corinth in early Christian times and making the ghost explicitly a vampire in his 1797 poem "The Bride of Corinth." The Goethe poem is appended here in full.

<110>

THE ORIGINAL OF THIS STORY

Philinnion was the daughter of Demostratus and Charito. She had been married to Craterus, Alexander's famous General, but had died six months after her marriage. As we learn that she was desperately in love with Machates, a foreign friend from Pella who had come to see Demostratus, the misery of her position may possibly have caused her death. But her love conquered death itself, and she returned to life again six months after she had died, and lived with Machates, visiting him for several nights. One day an old nurse went to the guest-chamber, and as the lamp was burning, she saw a woman sitting by Machates. Scarcely able to contain herself at this extraordinary occurrence, she ran to the girl's mother, calling: "Charito! Demostratus!" and bade them get up and go with her to their daughter, for by the grace of the gods she had appeared alive, and was with the stranger in the guest-chamber.

On hearing this extraordinary story, Charito was at first overcome by it and by the nurse's excitement; but she soon recovered herself, and burst into tears at the mention of her daughter, telling the old woman she was out of her senses, and ordering her out of the room. The nurse was indignant at this treatment, and boldly declared that she was not out of her senses, but that Charito was unwilling to see her daughter because she was afraid. At last Charito consented to go to the door of the guest-chamber, but as it was now quite two hours since she had heard the news, she arrived too late, and found them both asleep. The mother bent over the woman's figure, and thought she recognized her daughter's features and clothes. Not feeling sure, as it was dark, she decided to keep quiet for the present, meaning to get up early and catch the woman. If she failed, she would ask Machates for a full explanation, as he would never tell her a lie in a case so important. So she left the room without saying anything.

But early on the following morning, either because the gods so willed it or because she was moved by some divine impulse, the woman went away without being observed. When she came to him, Charito was angry with the young man in consequence, and clung to his knees, and conjured him to speak the truth and hide nothing from her. At first he was greatly distressed, and could hardly be brought to admit that the girl's name was Philinnion. Then he described her first coming and the violence of her passion, and told how she had said that she was there without her parents' knowledge. The better to establish the truth of his story, he opened a coffer and took out the things she had left behind her — a ring of gold which she had given him, and a belt which she had left on the previous night. When Charito beheld all these convincing proofs, she uttered a piercing cry, and rent her clothes and her cloak, and tore her coif from her head,

<111>

and began to mourn for her daughter afresh in the midst of her friends. Machates was deeply distressed on seeing what had happened, and how they were all mourning, as if for her second funeral. He begged them to be comforted, and promised them that they should see her if she appeared. Charito yielded, but bade him be careful how he fulfilled his promise.

When night fell and the hour drew near at which Philinnion usually appeared, they were on the watch for her. She came, as was her custom, and sat down upon the bed. Machates made no pretence, for he was genuinely anxious to sift the matter to the bottom, and secretly sent some slaves to call her parents. He himself could hardly believe that the woman who came to him so regularly at the same hour was really dead, and when she ate and drank with him, he began to suspect what had been suggested to him — namely, that some grave-robbers had violated the tomb and sold the clothes and the gold ornaments to her father.

Demostratus and Charito hastened to come at once, and when they saw her, they were at first speechless with amazement. Then, with cries of joy, they threw themselves upon their daughter. But Philinnion remained cold. "Father and mother," she said, "cruel indeed have ye been in that ye grudged my living with the stranger for three days in my father's house, for it brought harm to no one. But ye shall pay for your meddling with sorrow. I must return to the place appointed for me, though I came not hither without the will of Heaven." With these words she fell down dead, and her body lay stretched upon the bed. Her parents threw themselves upon her, and the house was filled with confusion and sorrow, for the blow was heavy indeed; but the event was strange, and soon became known throughout the town, and finally reached my ears.

During the night I kept back the crowds that gathered round the house, taking care that there should be no disturbance as the news spread. At early dawn the theatre was full. After a long discussion it was decided that we should go and open the tomb, to see whether the body was still on the bier, or whether we should find the place empty, for the woman had hardly been dead six months. When we opened the vault where all her family was buried, the bodies were seen lying on the other biers; but on the one where Philinnion had been placed, we found only the iron ring which had belonged to her lover and the gilt drinking-cup Machates had given her on the first day. In utter amazement, we went straight to Demostratus's house to see whether the body was still there. We beheld it lying on the ground, and then went in a large crowd to the place of assembly, for the whole event was of great importance and absolutely past belief. Great was the confusion, and no one could tell what to do, when Hyllus, who is not only considered the best diviner among us, but is also a great authority on the interpretation of the flight of birds, and is generally well versed in his art, got up and said that the woman must be buried

<112>

outside the boundaries of the city, for it was unlawful that she should be laid to rest within them; and that Hermes Chthonius and the Eumenides should be propitiated, and that all pollution would thus be removed. He ordered the temples to be re-consecrated and the usual rites to be performed in honour of the gods below. As for the King, in this affair, he privately told me to sacrifice to Hermes, and to Zeus Xenius, and to Ares, and to perform these duties with the utmost care. We have done as he suggested.

The stranger Machates, who was visited by the ghost, has committed suicide in despair.

—From Lacy Collison-Morley's *Greek and Roman Ghost Stories*

<113>

THE BRIDE OF CORINTH

GOETHE — Trans E.A. BOWRING[3]

Once a stranger youth to Corinth came,
Who in Athens lived, but hoped that he
From a certain townsman there might claim,
As his father's friend, kind courtesy.
Son and daughter, they
Had been wont to say
Should thereafter bride and bridegroom be.

But can he that boon so highly prized, .
Save 'tis dearly bought, now hope to get?
They are Christians and have been baptized,
He and all of his are heathens yet.
For a newborn creed,
Like some loathsome weed,
Love and truth to root out oft will threat.

Father, daughter, all had gone to rest,
And the mother only watches late;
She receives with courtesy the guest,
And conducts him to the room of state.
Wine and food are brought,
Ere by him besought
Bidding him good night. she leaves him straight.

But he feels no relish now, in truth
For the dainties so profusely spread;
Meat and drink forgets the wearied youth,
And, still dress'd, he lays him on the bed.
Scarce are closed his eyes,
When a form in-hies
Through the open door with silent tread.

---

[3] Edgar Alfred Bowring (1826-1911), *Poems of Goethe* (1853).

<114>

By his glimmering lamp discerns he now
How, in veil and garment white array'd,
With a black and gold band round her brow,
Glides into the room a bashful maid.
But she, at his sight,
Lifts her hand so white,
And appears as though full sore afraid.

"Am I," cries she, "such a stranger here,
That the guest's approach they could not name?
Ah, they keep me in my cloister drear,
Well nigh feel I vanquish'd by my shame.
On thy soft couch now
Slumber calmly thou!
"I'll return as swiftly as I came."

"Stay, thou fairest maiden!" cries the boy,
Starting from his couch with eager haste:
"Here are Ceres', Bacchus' gifts of joy;
Amor bringest thou, with beauty grac'd!
Thou art pale with fear!
Loved one let us here
Prove the raptures the Immortals taste."

"Draw not nigh, O Youth! afar remain!
Rapture now can never smile on me;
For the fatal step, alas! is ta'en,
Through my mother's sick-bed phantasy.
Cured, she made this oath:
'Youth and nature both
Shall henceforth to Heav'n devoted be.'

<115>

"From the house, so silent now, are driven
All the gods who reign'd supreme of yore;
One Invisible now rules in heaven,
On the cross a Saviour they adore.
Victims slay they here,
Neither lamb nor steer,
But the altars reek with human gore."⁴ —

And he lists, and ev'ry word he weighs,
While his eager soul drinks in each sound:
"Can it be that now before my gaze
Stands my loved one on this silent ground?
Pledge to me thy troth!
Through our father's oath:
With Heav'ns blessing will our love be crown'd." —

"Kindly youth, I never can be thine!
'Tis my sister they intend for thee.
When I in the silent cloister pine,
Ah, within her arms remember me!
Thee alone I love,
While love's pangs I prove
Soon the earth will veil my misery." —

"No! for by this glowing flame I swear,
Hymen hath himself propitious shown:
Let us to my father's house repair,
And thoult find that joy is not yet flown,
Sweetest, here then stay,
And without delay
Hold we now our wedding feast alone!"

---

⁴ *Human gore*. Goethe is mocking the trans-substantiation of bread and wine into the body and blood of Christ.

<116>

Then exchange they tokens of their truth;
She gives him a golden chain to wear,
And a silver chalice would the youth
Give her in return of beauty rare.
"That is not for me;
Yet I beg of thee,
One lock only give me of thy hair."

Now the ghostly hour of midnight knell'd,
And she seem'd right joyous at the sign;
To her pallid lips the cup she held,
But she drank of nought but blood-red wine.
For to taste the bread
There before them spread,
Nought he spoke could make the maid incline.

To the youth the goblet then she brought, —
He too quaff'd with eager joy the bowl.
Love to crown the silent feast he sought,
Ah! full love-sick was the stripling's soul.
From his prayer she shrinks,
Till at length he sinks
On the bed and weeps without control.

And she comes, and lays her near the boy:
"How I grieve to see thee sorrowing so!
If thou think'st to clasp my form with joy,
Thou must learn this secret sad to know;
Yes! the maid, whom thou
Call'st thy loved one now,
Is as cold as ice, though white as snow."

Then he clasps her madly in his arm,
While love's youthful might pervades his frame:
"Thou might'st hope, when with me, to grow warm.
E'en if from the grave thy spirit came!
Breath for breath, and kiss!
Overflow of bliss!
Dost not thou, like me, feel passion's flame?"

<117>

Love still closer rivets now their lips,
Tears they mingle with their rapture blest,
From his mouth the flame she wildly sips,
Each is with the other's thought possess'd.
His hot ardour's flood
Warms her chilly blood,
But no heart is beating in her breast.

In her care to see that nought went wrong,
Now the mother happen'd to draw near;
At the door long hearkens she, full long,
Wond'ring at the sounds that greet her ear.
Tones of joy and sadness,
And love's blissful madness,
As of bride and bridegroom they appear.

From the door she will not now remove
'Till she gains full certainty of this;
And with anger hears she vows of love,
Soft caressing words of mutual bliss.
"Hush! the cock's loud strain!
But thoult come again,
When the night returns!" — then kiss on kiss.

Then her wrath the mother cannot hold,
But unfastens straight the lock with ease
"In this house are girls become so bold,
As to seek e'en strangers' lusts to please?"
By her lamp's clear glow
Looks she in, — and oh!
Sight of horror! — 'tis her child she sees.

Fain the youth would, in his first alarm,
With the veil that o'er her had been spread,
With the carpet, shield his love from harm;
But she casts them from her, void of dread,
And with spirit's strength,
In its spectre length,
Lifts her figure slowly from the bed.

<118>

"Mother! mother!" — Thus her wan lips say:
"May not I one night of rapture share?
From the warm couch am I chased away?
Do I waken only to despair?
It contents not thee
To have driven me
An untimely shroud of death to wear?

"But from out my coffin's prison-bounds
By a wond'rous fate I'm forced to rove,
While the blessings and the chaunting sounds
That your priests delight in, useless prove.
Water, salt, are vain
Fervent youth to chain,
Ah, e'en Earth can never cool down love!

"When that infant vow of love was spoken,
Venus' radiant temple smiled on both.
Mother! thou that promise since hast broken,
Fetter'd by a strange, deceitful oath.
Gods, though, hearken ne'er,
Should a mother swear
To deny her daughter's plighted troth.

"From my grave to wander I am forc'd,
Still to seek The Good's long-sever'd link,
Still to love the bridegroom I have lost,
And the life-blood of his heart to drink;
When his race is run,
I must hasten on,
And the young must 'neath my vengeance sink.

"Beauteous youth! no longer mayst thou live;
Here must shrivel up thy form so fair;
Did not I to thee a token give,
Taking in return this lock of hair?
View it to thy sorrow!
Grey thoul't be to-morrow,
Only to grow brown again when there.

<119>

"Mother, to this final prayer give ear!
Let a funeral pile be straightway dress'd;
Open then my cell so sad and drear,
That the flames may give the lovers rest!
When ascends the fire
From the glowing pyre,
To the gods of old we'll hasten, blest."

<120>

The Grim White Woman

Original — M. G. LEWIS

Lord Ronald was handsome, Lord Ronald was young;
The green wood he traversed, and gaily he sung;
His bosom was light, and he spurred on amain,
When lo! a fair lass caught his steed by the rein.

She caught by the rein, and she sank on her knee;
— "Now stay thee, Lord Ronald, and listen to me!" —
She sank on her knee, and her tears 'gan to flow,
— "Now stay thee, Lord Ronald, and pity my woe!" —

— "Nay, Janet, fair Janet, I needs must away;
I speed to my mother, who chides my delay." —
— "Oh! heed not her chiding; though bitter it be,
Thy falsehood and scorn are more bitter to me." —

— "Nay, Janet, fair Janet, I needs must depart;
My brother stays for me to hunt the wild hart." —
— "Oh! let the hart live, and thy purpose forego,
To soothe with compassion and kindness my woe." —

— "Nay, Janet, fair Janet, delay me no more;
You please me no longer, my passion is o'er:
A leman[1] more lovely waits down in yon dell,
So, Janet, fair Janet, for ever farewell!" —

No longer the damsel's entreaties he heard;
His dapple-grey horse through the forest he spurr'd;
And ever, as onwards the foaming steed flew,
Did Janet with curses the false one pursue.

[1] *Leman*. Archaic word for *lover*.

<121>

— "Oh! cursed be the day," in distraction she cries,
"When first did thy features look fair in my eyes!
And cursed the false lips, which beguiled me of fame;
And cursed the hard heart, which resigns me to shame!

The wanton, whom now you forsake me to please —
May her kisses be poison, her touch be disease!
When you wed, may your couch be a stranger to joy,
And the Fiend of the Forest your offspring destroy!

May the Grim White Woman, who haunts this wood,
The Grim White Woman, who feasts on blood,
As soon as they number twelve months and a day,
Tear the hearts of your babes from their bosoms away." —

Then frantic with love and remorse home she sped,
Locked the door of her chamber, and sank on her bed;
Nor yet with complaints and with tears had she done,
When the clock in St. Christopher's church struck — "one!"

Her blood, why she knew not, ran cold at the sound;
She lifted her head; she gazed fearfully round!
When lo! near the hearth, by a cauldron's blue light,
She saw the tall form of a female in white.

Her eye, fixed and glassy, no passions express'd;
No blood filled her veins, and no heart warmed her breast!
She seemed like a corse[2] newly torn from the tomb,
And her breath spread the chillness of death through the room.

Her arms, and her feet, and her bosom were bare;
A shroud wrapped her limbs, and a snake bound her hair.
This spectre, the Grim White Woman was she,
And the Grim White Woman was fearful to see!

[2] *Corse.* Corpse.

<122>

And ever, the cauldron as over she bent,
She muttered strange words of mysterious intent:
A toad, still alive, in the liquor she threw,
And loud shrieked the toad, as in pieces it flew!

To heighten the charm, in the flames next she flung
A viper, a rat, and a mad tiger's tongue;
The heart of a wretch, on the rack newly dead,
And an eye, she had torn from a parricide's head.

The flames now divided; the charm was complete;
Her spells the White Spectre forbore to repeat;
To Janet their produce she hastened to bring,
And placed on her finger a little jet³ ring!

— "From the Grim White Woman," she murmured, "receive
A gift, which your treasure, now lost, will retrieve.
Remember, 'twas she who relieved your despair,
And when you next see her, remember your prayer!" —

This said, the Fiend vanished! no longer around
Poured the cauldron its beams; all was darkness profound;
Till the gay beams of morning illumined the skies,
And gay as the morning did Ronald arise.

With hawks and with hounds to the forest rode he:
— "Trallira! trallara! from Janet I'm free!
Trallira! trallara! my old love, adieu!
Trallira! trallara! I'll get me a new!" —

But while he thus carolled in bachelor's pride,
A damsel appeared by the rivulet's side:
He reined in his courser, and soon was aware,
That never was damsel more comely and fair.

³ *Jet.* A hard, intensely black gemstone, made from lignite, a quasi-mineral
related to coal. Used in monks' beads, bracelets, and jewellery.

<123>

He felt at her sight, what no words can impart;
She gave him a look, and he proffer'd his heart:
Her air, while she listen'd, was modest and bland:
She gave him a smile, and he proffered his hand.

Lord Ronald was handsome, Lord Ronald was young,
And soon on his bosom sweet Ellinor hung;
And soon to St. Christopher's chapel they ride,
And soon does Lord Ronald call Ellen his bride.

Days, weeks, and months fly. — "Ding-a-ding! ding-a-ding!" —
Hark! hark! in the air how the castle bells ring!
— "And why do the castle bells ring in the air?" —
Sweet Ellen hath borne to Lord Ronald an heir.

Days, weeks, and months fly. — "Ding-a-ding! ding-a-ding!"
Again, hark! how gaily the castle bells ring!
— "Why again do the castle bells carol so gay?" —
A daughter is born to Lord Ronald to-day.

But seest thou yon herald so swift hither bend?
Lord Ronald is summoned his king to defend;
And seest thou the tears of sweet Ellinor flow?
Lord Ronald has left her to combat the foe.

Where slumber her babies, her steps are addressed;
She presses in anguish her son to her breast;
Nor ceases she Annabell's cradle to rock,
Till — "one!" — is proclaimed by the loud castle clock.

Her blood, why she knows not, runs cold at the sound!
She raises her head; she looks fearfully round!
And lo! near the hearth, by a cauldron's blue light,
She sees the tall form of a female in white!

<124>

The female with horror sweet Ellen beholds:
Still closer her son to her bosom she folds;
And cold tears of terror bedew her pale cheeks,
While, nearer approaching, the Spectre thus speaks: —

— "The Grim White Woman, who haunts yon wood,
The Grim White Woman, who feasts on blood,
Since now he has numbered twelve months and a day,
Claims the heart of your son, and is come for her prey." —

— "Oh! Grim White Woman, my baby now spare!
I'll give you these diamonds so precious and fair!" —
— "Though fair be those diamonds, though precious they be,
The blood of thy babe is more precious to me!" —

— "Oh! Grim White Woman, now let my child live!
This cross of red rubies in guerdon[4] I'll give!"
"Though red be the flames from those rubies which dart,
More red is the blood of thy little child's heart." —

To soften the demon no pleading prevails;
The baby she wounds with her long crooked nails:
She tears from his bosom the heart as her prey!
— " 'Tis mine!" — shrieked the Spectre, and vanish'd away.

The foe is defeated, and ended the strife,
And Ronald speeds home to his children and wife.
Alas! on his castle a black banner flies,
And tears trickle fast from his fair lady's eyes.

— "Say, why on my castle a black banner flies,
And why trickle tears from my fair lady's eyes?" —
— "In your absence the Grim White Woman was here,
And dead is your son, whom you valued so dear." —

---

[4] *Guerdon*. Recompense or payment.

<125>

Deep sorrowed Lord Ronald; but soon for his grief,
He found in the arms of sweet Ellen relief:
Her kisses could peace to his bosom restore,
And the more he beheld her, he loved her the more;

Till it chanced, that one night, when the tempest was loud,
And strong gusts of wind rocked the turrets so proud,
As Ronald lay sleeping he heard a voice cry,
— "Dear father, arise, or your daughter must die!" —

He woke, gazed around, look'd below, look'd above;
— "Why trembles my Ronald? what ails thee, my love?" —
— "I dreamt, through the skies that I saw a hawk dart,
Pounce a little white pigeon, and tear out its heart." —

— "Oh! hush thee, my husband; thy vision was vain." —
Lord Ronald resigned him to slumber again:
But soon the same voice, which had roused him before,
Cried, — "Father, arise, or your daughter's no more!" —

He woke, gazed around, look'd below, look'd above;
— "What fears now, my Ronald? what ails thee, my love?" —
— "I dreamt that a tigress, with jaws open wide,
Had fastened her fangs in a little lamb's side!" —

— "Oh! hush thee, my husband; no tigress is here." —
Again Ronald slept, and again in his ear
Soft murmured the voice, — "Oh! be warn'd by your son;
Dear father, arise, for it soon will strike — 'one!' —

Your wife, for a spell your affections to hold,
To the Grim White Woman her children hath sold;
E'en now is the Fiend at your babe's chamber door;
Then, father, arise, or your daughter's no more!" —

<126>

From his couch starts Lord Ronald, in doubt and dismay,
He seeks for his wife — but his wife is away!
He gazes around, looks below, looks above;
Lo! there sits on his pillow a little white dove!

A mild lambent flame in its eyes seem'd to glow;
More pure was its plumage than still-falling snow,
Except where a scar could be seen on its side,
And three small drops of blood the white feathers had dyed.

— "Explain, pretty pigeon, what art thou, explain?" —
— "The soul of thy son, by the White Demon slain;
E'en now is the Fiend at your babe's chamber door,
And thrice having warned you, I warn you no more!" —

The pigeon then vanished; and seizing his sword,
The way to his daughter Lord Ronald explored;
Distracted he sped to her chamber full fast,
And the clock it struck — "one!" — as the threshold he past.

And straight near the hearth, by a cauldron's blue light,
He saw the tall form of a female in white;
Ellen wept, to her heart while her baby she press'd,
Whom the Spectre approaching, thus fiercely address'd:

— "The Grim White Woman, who haunts yon wood,
The Grim White Woman, who feasts on blood,
Since now she has numbered twelve months and a day,
Claims the heart of your daughter, and comes for her prey!" —

This said, she her nails in the child would have fix'd;
Sore struggled the mother; when, rushing betwixt,
Ronald struck at the Fiend with his ready-drawn brand,
And, glancing aside, his blow lopp'd his wife's hand!

<127>

Wild laughing, the Fiend caught the hand from the floor,
Releasing the babe, kissed the wound, drank the gore;
A little jet ring from the finger then drew,
Thrice shrieked a loud shriek, and was borne from their view!

Lord Ronald, while horror still bristled his hair,
To Ellen now turned — but no Ellen was there!
And lo! in her place, his surprise to complete,
Lay Janet, all covered with blood, at his feet!

— "Yes, traitor, 'tis Janet!" — she cried; "At my sight
"No more will your heart swell with love and delight;
That little jet ring was the cause of your flame,
And that little jet ring from the Forest-Fiend came.

"It endowed me with beauty, your heart to regain;
It fixed your affections, so wavering and vain;
But the spell is dissolved, and your eyes speak my fate,
My falsehood is clear, and as clear is your hate.

"But what caused *my* falsehood? — your falsehood alone;
What voice said, 'be guilty?' — seducer, your own!
You vowed truth for ever, the oath I believed,
And had *you* not deceived me, *I* had not deceived.

"Remember my joy, when affection you swore!
Remember my pangs, when your passion was o'er!
A curse, in my rage, on your children was thrown,
And alas! wretched mother, that curse struck my own!" —

And here her strength failed her! — the sad one to save
In vain the Leech⁵ labour'd; three days did she rave;
Death came on the fourth, and restored her to peace,
Nor long did Lord Ronald survive her decease.

⁵ *Leech*. Vulgar name for a physician, since doctors used leeches to bleed their patients.

<128>

Despair fills his heart! he no longer can bear
His castle, for Ellen no longer is there:
From Scotland[6] he hastens, all comfort disdains,
And soon his bones whiten on Palestine's[7] plains.

If you bid me, fair damsels, my moral rehearse,
It is, that young ladies ought never to curse;
For no one will think her well-bred, or polite,
Who devotes little babes to Grim Women in White.

[6] *Scotland*. This is the only place name that situates the poem geographically.
The absence of any other place names in the poem is striking.
[7] *Palestine*. This reference places the poem during one of the Crusades.

<129>

The Little Grey Man

Original — H[ENRY WILLIAM] BUNBURY[1]

[The siting of this poem in a precise locale and an exact period of history suggests that Bunbury may have read or heard local stories around Aix-la-Chapelle during his travels. The casual reader could mistake this poem for a Gothic concoction, a mere parody of "Alonzo the Brave," but in fact a close examination of a map of the region, and of the history of the Dutch-Spanish wars, suggest that Mary Ann's journey has some basis in real events, or is based on some Dutch or Flemish literary source as yet unidentified — BR].

Mary Ann[2] was the darling of Aix-la-Chapelle;[3]
She bore through its province, unenvied, the belle;
The joy of her fellows, her parents' delight;
So kind was her soul, and her beauty so bright:
No maiden surpassed, or perhaps ever can,
Of Aix-la-Chapelle the beloved Mary Ann.

Her form it was faultless, unaided by art;
And frank her demeanour, as guileless her heart;
Her soft melting eyes a sweet languor bedecked;
And youth's gaudy bloom was by love lightly checked;
On her mien had pure Nature bestowed her best grace,
And her mind stood confessed in the charms of her face.

---

1 *Bunbury*. Henry William Bunbury (1750-1811), British artist, sometimes called "The Second Hogarth," and "the most celebrated 'amateur' [caricaturist] of the eighteenth century" (Lynch 50). He was also known for a popular series of comic equestrian engravings, and serious engravings of scenes from Shakespeare. Many of his works appeared under the pseudonym "Geoffrey Gambado, Esq."
2 "Mary Anne" was a slang word for the guillotine. "Mary-Anne Associations" were secret French Republican societies. Mary-Ann, as a variant of Marian, also suggests the Virgin, and underscores the Catholic symbolism of the story.
3 *Aix-la-Chapelle*. Westphalian city noted for its hot springs, the burial place of Charlemagne and the site of coronations for German monarchs. In the 18th century, Aix-la-Chapelle was a spa city, infamous for prostitution, so a degree of irony can be inferred by having Mary-Ann a "belle" of a brothel town.

<130>

Portrait of Henry Bunbury as a youth, by Joshua Reynolds.

Though with suitors beset, yet her Leopold knew,
As her beauty was matchless, her heart it was true,
So fearless he went to the wars; while the maid,
Her fears for brave Leopold often betrayed:
Full oft, in the gloom of the churchyard reclined,
Would she pour forth her sorrows and vows to the wind.

— "Ah me!" — would she sigh, in a tone that would melt
The heart that one spark of true love ever felt;
— "Ah me!" — would she sigh, "past and gone is the day,
When my father was plighted to give me away!
My fancy, what sad gloomy presage appalls?
Ah! sure on the Danube my Leopold falls!"

<131>

One evening so gloomy, when only the owl
(A tempest impending) would venture to prowl;
Mary Ann, whose delight was in sadness and gloom,
By a newly made grave sat her down on a tomb;
But ere she to number her sorrows began,
Lo! out of the grave jumped a Little Grey Man!4

His hue it was deadly, his eyes they were ghast;
Long and pale were his fingers, that held her arm fast; —
She shrieked a loud shriek, so affrighted was she;
And grimly he scowled, as he jumped on her knee.
With a voice that dismayed her — "The Danube!" —
      he cried;
"There Leopold bleeds! Mary Ann is my bride!" —

She shrunk, all appalled, and she gazed all around;
She closed her sad eyes, and she sunk on the ground;
The Little Grey Man he resumed his discourse —
— "To-morrow I take thee, for better, for worse: —
At midnight my arms shall thy body entwine,
Or this newly made grave, Mary Ann, shall be thine!" —

With fear and with fright did the maid look around,
When she first dared to raise her sad eyes from the ground;
With fear and with fright gazed the poor Mary Ann,
Though lost to her sight was the Little Grey Man:
With fear and with fright from the churchyard she fled;
Reached her home, now so welcome, and sunk on her bed.

---

4 "Little Grey Man." Since the protagonists of this poem are all Catholic, the
Calvinist Protestants of northern Holland are the villains and oppressors. It is
not far off the mark to characterize a Dutch Calvinist as a "little grey man." The
resemblance to various "temptation" stories involving Satan or demons is not
coincidental. Figures in gray also occasionally turn up in fairy stories.
It is also possible that the Little Grey Man is a caricature of Lewis — reverse
Lewis's initials, MGL, and they become LGM, for Little Grey Man. Lewis was
held up to frequent ridicule in polite society, and was described as one of the
shortest men in England. Since Bunbury illustrated the parody-sequel to *Tales of
Wonder*, *Tales of Terror*, he is clearly involved, in 1801, in the mockery of Lewis.
The earliest reference I have found to "The Little Grey Man," which was
published in a periodical anonymously, is in April 1798, at the peak of Lewis's
notoriety as Gothic novelist and playwright.

<132>

— "Woe is me!" did she cry — "that I ever was born!
Was ever poor maiden so lost and forlorn!
Must that Little Grey Man, then, my body entwine,
Or the grave newly dug for another be mine?
Shall I wait for to-morrow's dread midnight? — ah, no!
To my Leopold's arms — to the Danube — I go!"

Then up rose the maiden, so sore woe-begone,
And her Sunday's apparel in haste she put on;
Her close studded bodice of velvet so new;
Her coat of fine scarlet, and kirtle of blue;
Her ear-rings of jet, all so costly; and last,
Her long cloak of linsey,⁵ to guard from the blast.

A cross of pure gold, her fond mother's bequest,
By a still dearer ribbon she hung at her breast;
Round a bodkin of silver she bound her long hair,
In plaits and in tresses so comely and fair,
'Twould have gladdened your heart, ere her journey began,
To have gazed on the tidy and trim Mary Ann.

But, oh! her sad bosom such sorrows oppressed,
Such fears and forebodings, as robbed her of rest;
Forlorn as she felt, so forlorn must she go,
And brave the rough tempest, the hail, and the snow!
Yet still she set forth, all so pale and so wan —
Let a tear drop of pity for poor Mary Ann.

Dark, dark was the night, and the way it was rude;
While the Little Grey Man on her thoughts would obtrude;
She wept as she thought on her long gloomy way;
She turned, and she yet saw the lights all so gay:
She kissed now her cross, as she heard the last bell;
And a long, long adieu bade to Aix-la-Chapelle.

---

⁵ *Linsey.* Linsey-woolsey, a coarse fabric of intertwined linen and wool. It is
fascinating that Mary-Ann, rather than disguising herself as a man, a tradition in
romance, would dress herself up in costly attire, as for a wedding, so that she
could pass unscathed through wilderness, amid bandits. Gothic indeed.
Fortunately for Mary-Ann, high heels had not yet been invented.

<133>

Through the brown wood of Limbourg[6] with caution[7] she paced;
Ere the noon of the morrow she traversed the waste;
She mounted the hills of St. Bertrand[8] so high;
And the day it declined, as the heath she drew nigh;
And she rested a wide-waving alder beneath,
And paused on the horrors of Sombermond's heath:[9]

For there, in black groups (by the law 'tis imposed),
Are the bodies of fell malefactors exposed,
On wheels and on gibbets, on crosses and poles,
With a charge to the passing, to pray for their souls;
But a spot of such terror no robbers infest,
And there the faint pilgrim securely may rest.

Sore fatigued, the sad maid knelt, and said a short prayer;
She bound up her tresses, that flow'd in the air:
Again she set forth, and sped slowly along;
And her steps tried to cheer, but in vain, with a song:
In her thoughts all so gloomy, sad presages ran,
Of Leopold now, now the Little Grey Man.

---

[6] Limbourg/Limburg was in Belgium in Lewis's time. It is now part of Holland.
It was a Roman settlement and, like Aix-la-Chapelle, site of hot springs. A
Roman bath (thermae) is preserved there.

[7] *With caution* – In the 18th century, the area around Limburg was infamous for
the activities of bandit gangs — actually guerillas resisting Protestant rule —
called "goat riders." During the more remote period alluded to in this poem –
the wars against Spain and the Habsburgs ending in 1713 — similar groups of
bandits and outlaws would have been even more common.

[8] *St. Bertrand*. There is a place called St. Bertrand, a village in the Pyrenees, site
of a Gothic cathedral, but this is too remote from the setting of this poem. It is
possible that one of the hills in the highlands of Haute Fagnes once had a shrine
to St. Bertrand, or that this is simply a fanciful place name interpolated by the
poet.

[9] *Sombermond's heath*. The heath would almost certainly be in the Haute Fagnes
(High Fens), a vast wasteland of moorland, swamp and forest. I did not locate a
place or hall called Sombermond, but the name Suermondt occurs as a family
name in Aix-la-Chapelle. That city's museum is the Suermondt-Ludwig
museum. Mary Ann's journey could easily have taken her to the Haute Fagnes.

<134>

The moon dimly gleamed as she enter'd the plain;
The winds swept the clouds rolling on to the main;
For a hut e'er so wretched in vain she look'd round;
No tree promised shelter, no bed the cold ground:
Her limbs they now faulter'd, her courage all fled,
As a faint beam displayed the black groups of the dead.

Shrill whistled the wind through the skulls, and the blast
Scared the yet greedy bird from its glutting repast;
From the new-rack'd assassin[10] the raven withdrew,
But croak'd round the wheel still, and heavily flew;
While vultures, more daring, intent on their prey,
Tore the flesh from the sinews, yet reeking, away.

But the dread of banditti, some strength it restored;
And again she the aid of the Virgin implored;
She dragged her slow steps to where corses, yet warm,
Threw their tattered and fresh mangled limbs to the storm:
She reached the fell spot, and aghast, looking round,
At a black gibbet's foot senseless sunk on the ground.

Now the battle was over, and o'er his proud foes
The Austrian eagle[11] triumphantly rose;
'Midst the groans of the dying, and blood of the slain,
Sorely wounded lay Leopold, stretched on the plain.
When reviving, he first to look round him began,
Lo! close by his side sat a Little Grey Man!

[10] *Assassin.* The executed persons were almost certainly Protestants, although any mercenary soldier might also be termed an "assassin" by his enemies. The vast majority of soldiers in European wars at this period were mercenaries.
[11] *Austrian eagle.* At some point in the wars, the Austrian branch of the Hapsburgs took over from the Spanish. It is not clear from the text whether Leopold fought for the Spanish/Austrian side, but as a Catholic, he almost certainly would have.

<135>

The Little Grey Man he sat munching a heart,
And he growled in a tone all dismaying — "Depart!
Don't disturb me at meals! pri'thee rise, and pass on!
To Mary Ann hie! bind your wounds, and begone!
In a score and three days shall you meet Mary Ann;
And perhaps, uninvited, the Little Grey Man." —

With fear and dismay rose the youth from the ground,
His wounds he with balms and with bandages bound;
To quit his grim guest he made little delay,
And, faint though he was, he sped willing away:
For a score and three days did he journey amain,
Then sunk, all exhausted, on Sombermond's plain.

By the screams of the night-bird, though dark, he could tell
'Twas the gibbets amongst, and the wheels, where he fell. —
Now still her sad station did Mary Ann keep,
Where Leopold, fainting, had sunk into sleep:
Ah! little thought he that his dear one was by!
Ah! little the maid that her love was so nigh!

Perched grim on a wheel sat the Little Grey Man,
Whilst his fierce little eyes o'er the sad lovers ran;
The Little Gray Man down to Leopold crept,
And opened his wounds, all so deep, as he slept;
With a scream he the slumbers of Mary Ann broke,
And the poor forlorn maid to new horrors awoke.

To her sight, sorely shocked, did a moonbeam display
Her lover, all bleeding and pale as he lay:
She shrieked a loud shriek; and she tore her fine hair,
And she sunk her soft cheek on his bosom so fair;
With her long flowing tresses she strove to restrain,
And stop the dear blood that now issued amain.

<136>

To his wounds her fair hands she unceasingly pressed;
Her tears fast they fell on her Leopold's breast;
Entranced, and in slumber still silent he lay,
Till the Little Grey Man drove his slumbers away;
With a vision all horrid his senses betrayed,
And fatal to him and his much-beloved maid.

He dreamt, from his wheel an assassin had stepp'd,
And silent and slowly had close to him crept;
That the wretch, mangled piecemeal, and ghastly with gore,
From his wounds both the balms and the bandages tore;
And to search for his dagger as now he began,
— "Strike! strike!" cried the voice of the Little Grey Man.

"Strike! strike!" cried the fiend, "or your wounds bleed anew!"
He struck — it was Mary Ann's life-blood he drew —
With a shriek he awoke, nor his woes were they o'er;
He beheld his pale love, to behold her no more!
Her eyes the poor maiden on Leopold cast,
Gave him one look of love, 'twas her fondest, her last![12]

The Little Grey Man now he set up a yell,
Which was heard in the halls of fair Aix-la-Chapelle,
He raised up his head, and he raised up his chin;
And he grinned, as he shouted, a horrible grin;
And he laughed a loud laugh, and his cap up he cast,
Exulting, as breathed the fond lovers their last.

As in each other's arms dead the fond lovers fell,
O'er the black lonely heath tolled a low, distant bell;
From the gibbets and crosses shrieks issued, and groans,
And wild to the blast flew the skulls and the bones;
Whilst the Little Grey Man, 'midst a shower of blood,
In a whirlwind was hurled into Sombermond's wood.

---

[12] This horrible outcome stands well as an indictment of the sectarian madness
that swept Europe for hundreds of years. The Grey Man revels in seeing his
enemies thus undone. The sometime wars between Spain and France come to
mind here, a delight to Protestant nations.

<137>

Of Mary Ann's sorrows, and Leopold's woes,
Long shall Maise's[13] dark stream tell the tale as it flows:
Long, long shall the gossips of Aix-la-Chapelle,
Of the heath and its horrors, the traveller tell;
Who shall prick on his steed with what swiftness he can,
Lest he meet in the twilight the Little Grey Man.

On the Feast of St. Austin,[14] to Sombermond's fair
Flock the youth of both sexes, its revels to share;
And in dainty apparel, all gallant and gay,
With dance, and with carols, and mirth, cheer the day;
While the proud castle's[15] portal expanded, invites
To the hall's ample board, and its festive delights:

And there, on the richly wrought arras, they view
Depicted, the woes of these lovers so true;
The troubles their sorrowful days that befell,
And the fate of the darling of Aix-la-Chapelle;
Behold, as she bloomed, the beloved Mary-Ann,
And the heart-freezing scowl of the Little Grey Man.

---

13 Maise. Meuse river. Five regional rivers have their origin in the Hautes Fagnes region.

14 *St. Austin*. St. Augustine of Canterbury. His feast day is May 27.

15 The locale has shifted back to Aix-la-Chapelle, and the castle can only be the 14th century Frankenberg castle, where, perhaps, Bunbury saw a tapestry or painting suggesting this story. French-made tapestries of the 1700s reached a pinnacle of detail and shading, achieving a palette of over a thousand colors. Flemish weaver Judocus de Vos (1661-1734), produced tapestries illustrated with events from the War of the Spanish Succession. Thus, Bunbury's poem could well be in the grand tradition of ekphrastic poetry.

<138>

Glenfinlas; or, Lord Ronald's Coronach[1]

Original.   WALTER SCOTT

"For them the viewless forms of air obey,
Their bidding heed, and at their beck repair:
   They know what spirit brews the stormful day,
And heartless oft, like moody madness, stare
To see the phantom train their secret work prepare."[2]

O hone a rie! O hone a rie![3]
   The pride of Albin's line is o'er
And fallen Glenartney's stateliest tree,—
   We ne'er shall see Lord Ronald more!

Oh, sprung from great Macgilliannore,
   The chief that never feared a foe,
How matchless was thy broad claymore,
   How deadly thine unerring bow.

Well can the *Saxon*[4] widows tell
   How, on the Tieth's resounding shore,
The boldest Lowland warriors fell,
   As down from Lenny's Pass you bore.

---

[1] *Glenfinlas* is a tract of forest ground lying in the Highlands of Perthshire, not far from Callender, in Menteith. To the west of the forest of Glenfinlas lies Loch Katrine, and its romantic avenue, called the Trossachs. Benledi, Benmore, and Benvoirlich, are mountains in the same district, and at no great distance from Glenfinlas. The river Teith passes Callender and the castle of Doune, and joins the Forth near Stirling. The Pass of Lenny is immediately above Callender, and is the principal access to the Highlands, from that town. Glenartney is a forest near Benvoirlich. The whole forms a sublime tract of Alpine scenery —WS.
[2] From William Collins (1721-1750), "An Ode on the Popular Superstitions of the Highlands of Scotland, Considered as the Subject of Poetry." (1750) ll. 65-69 —BR.
[3] *Coronach* is the lamentation for a deceased warrior, sung by the aged of the clan. *O hone a rie* signifies—"Alas! for the prince or chief" —WS.
[4] *Saasenach*. The term Sassenach, or Saxon, is applied by the Highlanders to their Low-country neighbours —WS.

<139>

But in his halls, on festal day,
    How blazed Lord Ronald's *beltane*[5] tree;
While youths and maids the light strathspey
    So nimbly danced with Highland glee.

Cheered by the strength of Ronald's shell,
    E'en age forgot his tresses hoar;
But now the loud lament we swell,
    Oh, ne'er to see Lord Ronald more!

From distant isles a chieftain came,
    The joys of Ronald's halls to find,
And chase with him the dark brown game
    That bounds o'er Albin's hills of wind.

'Twas Moy; whom in Columba's isle
    The Seer's prophetic spirit[6] found,
As with a minstrel's fire the while
    He waked his harp's harmonious sound.

Full many a spell to him was known,
    Which wandering spirits shrink to hear,
And many a lay of potent tone
    Was never meant for mortal ear.

For there, 'tis said, in mystic mood
    High converse with the dead they hold,
And oft espy the fated shroud
    That shall the future corpse enfold.

---

5 *Beltane-tree;* the fires lighted by the Highlanders on the first of May [Beltane], in compliance with a custom derived from the Pagan times, are so called. It is a festival celebrated with various superstitious rites both in the north of Scotland and in Wales —WS.

6 *Seer's spirit.* I can only describe the second sight, by adopting Dr. Johnson's definition, who calls it — "An impression either by the mind upon the eye, or by the eye upon the mind, by which things distant and future are perceived and seen if they were present." To which I would only add, that the spectral appearances thus presented, usually presage misfortune; that the faculty is painful to those who suppose they possess it; and that they usually acquire it while themselves under the pressure of melancholy — WS.

<140>

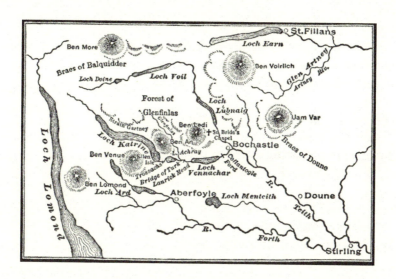

Oh, so it fell, that on day,
   To rouse the red deer from their den,
The chiefs have ta'en their distant way,
   And scoured the deep Glenfinlas glen.

No vassals wait their sports to aid,
   To watch their safety, deck their board,
Their simple dress, the Highland plaid;
   Their trusty guard, the Highland sword.

Three summer days, through brake and dell
   Their whistling shafts successful flew,
And still, when dewy evening fell,
   The quarry to their hut they drew.

In grey Glenfinlas' deepest nook
   The solitary cabin stood,
Fast by Moneira's sullen brook,
   Which murmurs through that lonely wood.

<141>

Soft fell the night, the sky was calm,
　　When three successive days had flown,
And summer mist, in dewy balm,
　　Steeped heathy bank and mossy stone.

The moon, half hid in silvery flakes,
　　Afar her dubious radiance shed,
Quivering on Katrine's distant lakes,
　　And resting on Benledi's head.

Now in their hut, in social guise,
　　Their sylvan fare the chiefs enjoy,
And pleasure laughs in Ronald's eyes,
　　As many a pledge he quaffs to Moy.

"What lack we here to crown our bliss,
　　While thus the pulse of joy beats high,
What but fair woman's yielding kiss,
　　Her panting breath, and melting eye?

"To chase the deer of yonder shades,
　　This morning left their father's pile
The fairest of our mountain maids,
　　The daughters of the proud Glengyle.

"Long have I sought sweet Mary's heart,
　　And dropped the tear, and heaved the sigh;
But vain the lover's wily art,
　　Beneath a sister's watchful eye.

"But thou mayst teach that guardian fair,
　　While far with Mary I am flown,
Of other hearts to cease her care,
　　And find it hard to guard her own.

<142>

"Touch but thy harp, thou soon shalt see
    The lovely Flora of Glengyle,
Unmindful of her charge, and me,
    Hang on thy notes 'twixt tear and smile.

"Or if she choose a melting tale,
    All underneath the greenwood bough,
Will good St. Oran's[7] rule prevail,
    Stern huntsman of the rigid vow?" —

"Since Enrick's fight, since Morna's death,
    No more on me shall rapture rise,
Responsive to the panting breath,
    Or yielding kiss, or melting eyes.

"E'en then, when o'er the heath of woe,
    Where sunk my hopes of love and fame,
I bade my harp's wild wailings flow,
    On me the Seer's sad spirit came.

"The last dread curse of angry Heaven,
    With ghastly sights, and sounds of woe,
To dash each glimpse of joy was given,
    The gift, the future ill to know.

"The bark thou saw'st yon summer morn
    So gaily part from Lulan's bay,
My eye beheld her dashed and torn
    Far on the rocky Colensay.

"The Fergus too — thy sister's son,
    Thou saw'st with pride the gallant's power,
As, marching 'gainst the Laird of Doune,
    He left the skirts of huge Benmore.

---

[7] *St. Oran*. A friend and follower of St. Columbus; he was buried in Icolmkill.
—WS

<143>

"Thou only saw'st his banners wave,
    As down Benvoirlich's side they wound,
Heard'st but the pibroch[8] answering brave
    To many a target clanking round.

"I heard the groans, I marked the tears,
    I saw the wound his bosom bore,
When on the serried Saxon spears
    He poured his clan's resistless roar.

"And thou who bidst me think of bliss,
    And bidst my heart awake to glee,
And court, like thee, the wanton kiss,
    That heart, O Ronald, bleeds for thee!

"I see the death damps chill thy brow,
    I hear the warning spirit cry;
The corpse-lights dance — they're gone, and now. . . .
    No more is given to gifted eye!" —

"Alone enjoy the dreary dreams,
    Sad prophet of the evil hour;
Say, should we scorn joy's transient beams,
    Because to-morrow's storm may lour?

"Or sooth, or false thy words of woe,
    Clangillan's chieftain ne'er shall fear;
His blood shall bound at rapture's glow,
    Though doomed to stain the Saxon spear.

"E'en now, to meet me in yon dell,
    My Mary's buskins brush the dew."
He spoke, nor bade the chief farewell,
    But called his dogs, and gay withdrew.

---

[8] *Pibroch*. A piece of martial music adapted to the Highland bagpipes. —WS

<144>

Within an hour returned each hound,
    In rushed the rousers of the deer;
They howled in melancholy sound,
    Then closely couched beside the Seer.

No Ronald yet — though midnight came,
    And sad were Moy's prophetic dreams,
As bending o'er the dying flame
    He fed the watch-fire's quivering gleams.

Sudden the hounds erect their ears,
    And sudden cease their moaning howl;
Close pressed to Moy, they mark their fears
    By shivering limbs, and stifled growl.

Untouched the harp began to ring,
    As softly, slowly, opened the door,
And shook responsive every string,
    As light a footstep pressed the floor.

And by the watch-fire's glimmering light,
    Close by the minstrel's side was seen
A huntress maid, in beauty bright,
    All dropping wet her robes of green.

All dropping wet her garments seem,
    Chilled was her cheek, her bosom bare,
As bending o'er the dying gleam,
    She wrung the moisture from her hair.

With maiden blush she softly said,
    "O gentle huntsman, hast thou seen,
In deep Glenfinlas' moon-light glade,
    A lovely maid in vest of green:

<145>

"With her a chief in Highland pride,
    His shoulders bear the hunter's bow;
The mountain dirk adorns his side,
    Far on the wind his tartans flow?" —

"And who art thou; and who are they?"
    All ghastly gazing, Moy replied;
"And why, beneath the moon's pale ray,
    Dare ye thus roam Glenfinlas' side?" —

"Where wild Loch Katrine pours her tide
    Blue, dark, and deep, round many an isle,
Our father's towers o'erhang her side,
    The castle of the bold Glengyle.

"To chase the dun Glenfinlas deer,
    Our woodland course this morn we bore,
And haply met, while wandering here,
    The son of great Macgilliannore.

"Oh, aid me then to seek the pair,
    When loitering in the woods I lost;
Alone I dare not venture there,
    Where walks, they say, the shrieking ghost." —

"Yes, many a shrieking ghost walks there;
    Then first, my own sad vow to keep,
Here will I pour my midnight prayer,
    Which still must rise when mortals sleep." —

"Oh, first, for pity's gentle sake,
    Guide a lone wanderer on her way,
For I must cross the haunted brake,
    And reach my father's towers ere day." —

<146>

"First three times tell each Ave-bead,
    And thrice a Paternoster say,
Then kiss with me the holy reed,
    So shall we safely wind our way." —

"Oh, shame to knighthood strange and foul!
    Go doff the bonnet from thy brow,
And shroud thee in the monkish cowl,
    Which best befits thy sullen vow.

"Not so, by high Dunlathmon's fire,
    Thy heart was froze to faith and joy,
When gaily rung thy raptured lyre,
    To wanton Morna's melting eye." —

Wild stared the Minstrel's eyes of flame,
    And high his sable locks arose,
And quick his colour went and came,
    As fear and rage alternate rose.

"And thou! when by the blazing oak
    I lay to her and love resigned,
Say, rode ye on the eddying smoke,
    Or sailed ye on the midnight wind?

"Not thine a race of mortal blood,
    Nor old Glengyle's pretended line;
Thy dame, the Lady of the Flood,
    Thy sire, the Monarch of the Mine."

He muttered thrice St. Oran's rhyme,
    And thrice St. Fillan's[9] powerful prayer,
Then turned him to the Eastern clime,
    And sternly shook his coal-black hair;

9 *St. Fillan.* I know nothing of St. Fillan, but that he has given his name to many chapels, holy fountains, &c., in Scotland. —WS [St. Fillan is an obscure Irish-born saint who settled in Scotland. His saintly powers include healing the sick, and he is reputed to have one phosphorescent arm, by whose light he can read and write in the darkness of monks' cells. St. Fillan is also the patron saint of the insane —BR.]

<147>

And bending o'er his harp, he flung
    His wildest witch-notes on the wind,
And loud, and high, and strange they rung,
    As many a magic change they find.

Tall waxed the Spirit's altering form,
    Till to the roof her stature grew,
Then mingling with the rising storm,
    With one wild yell away she flew.

Rain beats, hail rattles, whirlwinds tear,
    The slender hut in fragments flew,
But not a lock of Moy's loose hair,
    Was waved by wind, or wet by dew.

Wild mingling with the howling gale,
    Loud bursts of ghastly laughter rise,
High o'er the Minstrel's head they sail,
    And die amid the northern skies.

The voice of thunder shook the wood,
    As ceased the more than mortal yell,
And spattering foul a shower of blood,
    Upon the hissing firebands fell.

Next dropped from high a mangled arm,
    The fingers strained a half-drawn blade:
And last, the life-blood streaming warm,
    Torn from the trunk, a gasping head.

Oft o'er that head in battling field,
    Streamed the proud crest of high Benmore;
That arm the broad claymore could wield,
    Which dyed the Teith with Saxon Gore.

<148>

Woe to Moneira's sullen rills!
  Woe to Glenfinlas' dreary glen!
There never son of Albin's hills
  Shall draw the hunter's shaft agen!

E'en the tired pilgrim's burning feet
  At noon shall shun that sheltering den,
Lest, journeying in their rage, he meet
  The wayward Ladies of the Glen.

And we — behind the chieftain's shield
  No more shall we in safety dwell;
None leads the people to the field —
  And we the loud lament must swell.

O hone a rie! O hone a rie!
  The pride of Albin's line is o'er;
And fallen Glenartney's stateliest tree,
  We ne'er shall see Lord Ronald more!*

*The simple tradition upon which the preceding stanzas are
founded, runs as follows. While two Highland hunters were passing
the night in a solitary bathy (a hut built for the purpose of hunting),
and making merry over their venison and whisky, one of them
expressed a wish that they had pretty lasses to complete their party.
The words were scarcely uttered, when two beautiful young women,
habited in green, entered the hut, dancing and singing. One of the
hunters was seduced by the siren who attached herself particularly
to him, to leave the hut: the other remained, and, suspicious of the
fair seducers, continued to play upon a trump, or jew's-harp, some
strain consecrated to the Virgin Mary. Day at length came, and the
temptress vanished. Searching the forest, he found the bones of his
unfortunate friend, who had been torn to pieces and devoured by
the Fiend into whose toils he had fallen. The place was, from thence,
called the Glen of the Green Women —WS.

<149>

The Eve of St. John

Original. WALTER SCOTT

Smaylho'me, Smallholm Tower, the scene of the following Ballad, is situated on the northern boundary of Roxburghshire, among a cluster of wild rocks, called Sandiknow Crags, the property of Hugh Scott, Esq., of Harden. The tower is a high square building, surrounded by an outer wall, now ruinous. The circuit of the outer court being defended, on three sides, by a precipice and morass, is only accessible, from the west, by a steep and rocky path. The apartments, as usual, in a Border Keep, or fortress, are placed one above another, and communicate by a narrow stair; on the roof are two bartizans, or platforms, for defence or pleasure. The inner door of the tower is wood, the outer an iron grate; the distance between them being nine feet, the thickness, namely, of the wall. From the elevated situation of Smaylho'me Tower, it is seen many miles in every direction. Among the crags by which it is surrounded, one more eminent is called the "Watchfold," and is said to have been the station of a beacon in the times of war with England. Without the tower-court is a ruined Chapel.

The Baron of Smaylho'me rose with day,
 He spurred his courser on,
Without stop or stay, down the rocky way
 That leads to Brotherstone.

He went not with the bold Buccleuch,
 His banner broad to rear;
He went not 'gainst the English yew
 To lift the Scottish spear.

Yet his plate-jack[1] was braced, and his helmet was laced,
 And his vaunt-brace of proof he wore;
At his saddle-girth was a good steel sperthe,
 Full ten pound weight and more.

---

[1] The plate-jack is coat armour; the vaunt-brace (avant-bras), armour for the shoulders and arms: the sperthe, a battle-axe —WS.

<150>

The Baron returned in three days' space,
    And his looks were sad and sour,
And weary was his courser's pace
    As he reached his rocky tower.

He came not from where Ancram Moor[2]
    Ran red with English blood,
Where the Douglas true, and the bold Buccleuch,
    'Gainst keen Lord Ivers stood;

Yet was his helmet hacked and hewed,
    His acton pierced and tore;
His axe and his dagger with blood embrued,
    But it was not English gore.

He lighted at the Chapellage,
    He held him close and still,
And he whistled twice for his little foot-page,
    His name was *English Will.*

"Come thou hither, my little foot-page,
    Come hither to my knee,
Though thou art young, and tender of age,
    I think thou art true to me.

"Come, tell me all that thou hast seen,
    And look thou tell me true;
Since I from Smaylho'me Tower have been,
    What did thy lady do?"

"My lady, each night, sought the lonely light,
    That burns on the wild *Watchfold;*
For from height to height, the beacons bright,
    Of the English foemen told.

---

2 *Ancram Moor.* A.D. 1555, was fought the battle of Ancram Moor, in which
Archibald Douglas Earl of Angus, and Sir Walter Scott of Buccleuch, routed a
superior English army, under Lord Ralph Ivers, and Sir Brian Latoun —WS.

<151>

"The bittern clamoured from the moss,
    The wind blew loud and shrill,
Yet the craggy pathway she did cross
    To the eiry[3] beacon hill.

"I watched her steps, and silent came
    Where she sate her on a stone;
No watchman stood by the dreary flame,
    It burned all alone.

"The second night I kept her in sight,
    Till to the fire she came;
And by Mary's might, an armed knight
    Stood by the lonely flame.

"And many a word that warlike lord
    Did speak to my lady there,
But the rain fell fast, and loud blew the blast,
    And I heard not what they were.

"The third night there the sky was fair,
    And the mountain blast was still,
As again I watched the secret pair,
    On the lonesome beacon hill;

"And I heard her name the midnight hour,
    And name this holy eve;
And say, come that night to thy lady's bower;
    Ask no bold Baron's leave.

"He lifts his spear with the bold Buccleuch,
    His lady is alone;
The door she'll undo, to her knight so true,
    On the eve of good St. John."[4]

---

[3] *Eiry* is a Scotch expression signifying the feeling inspired by the dread of apparitions —WS.
[4] *St. John's Eve,* or Midsummer Eve (June 23), is associated with magic and fairy lore throughout Europe. The brevity of the summer night, the year's shortest, is said to provoke a particular frenzy among witches and spirits.

<152>

"I cannot come, I must not come,
    I dare not come to thee;
On the eve of St. John I must wander alone,
    In thy bower I may not be."

"Now out on thee, faint-hearted knight!
    Thou shouldst not say me nay,
For the eve is sweet, and when lovers meet,
    Is worth the whole summer's day.

"And I'll chain the bloodhound, and warder shall not sound,
    And rushes shall be strewed on the stair,
So by the rood-stone,⁵ and by holy St. John,
    I conjure thee, my love, to be there."

"Though the bloodhound be mute, and the rush beneath my foot,
    And the warder his bugle should not blow,
Yet there sleepeth a priest in the chamber to the east,
    And my footstep he would know."

"Oh, fear not the priest who sleepeth to the east,
    For to Dryburgh⁶ the way he hath ta'en:
And there to say mass, till three days to pass,
    For the soul of a knight that is slain."

"He turned him around, and grimly he frowned,
    Then he laughed right scornfully —
—'He who says the mass rite, for the soul of that knight,
    May as well say mass for me.

At the lone midnight hour, when bad Spirits have power,
    In thy chamber will I be.' —
With that he was gone, and my lady left alone,
    And no more did I see."

---

⁵ *The Black Rood* of Melrose was a crucifix of black marble, and of superior sanctity —WS.
⁶ Dryburgh Abbey is beautifully situated on the banks of the Tweed. After its dissolution it became the property of the Haliburtons of Newmains, and is now the seat of the Right Honourable the Earl of Buchan —WS.

<153>

Then changed, I trow, was that bold Baron's brow,
    From dark to blood-red high.
"Now tell me the mien of the knight thou hast seen,
    For, by Mary, he shall die!" —

"His arms shone full bright, in the beacon's red light,
    His plume it was scarlet and blue;
On his shield was a hound in a silver leash bound,
    And his crest was a branch of the yew." —

"Thou liest, thou liest, thou little foot-page,
    Loud dost thou lie to me;
For that knight is cold, and low laid in the mould,
    All under the Eildon[7] tree." —

"Yet hear but my word, my noble lord,
    For I heard her name his name;
And that lady bright she called the knight
    Sir Richard of Coldinghame." —

The bold Baron's brow then changed, I trow,
    From high blood-red to pale.
"The grave is deep and dark, and the corpse is stiff and stark;
    So I may not trust thy tale.

"Where fair Tweed flows round holy Melrose,
    And Eildon slopes to the plain,
Full three nights ago, by some secret foe,
    That gallant knight was slain.

"The varying light deceived thy sight,
    And the wild winds drowned the name,
For the Dryburgh bells ring, and the white monks they sing,
    For Sir Richard of Coldinghame."

---

[7] *Eildon* is a high hill, terminating in three conical summits, immediately above
the town of Melrose, where are the admired ruins of a magnificent monastery.
Eildon-tree was said to be the spot where Thomas the Rhymer uttered his
prophecies — WS.

<154>

He passed the court-gate, and he oped the tower grate,
　　And he mounted the narrow stair,
To the bartizan-seat, where, with maids that on her wait,
　　He found his lady fair.

That lady sat in mournful mood,
　　Looked over hill and vale,
Over Tweed's fair flood, and Merton's wood,
　　And all down Teviotdale.

— "Now hail! now hail! thou lady bright!" —
— "Now hail! thou Baron true!
What news, what news from Ancram fight?
　　What news from the bold Buccleuch?" —

—"The Ancram Moor is red with gore,
　　For many a Southern fell;
And Buccleuch has charged us evermore,
　　To watch our beacons well." —

The lady blushed red, but nothing she said,
　　Nor added the Baron a word;
Then she stepped down the stair to her chamber fair,
　　And so did her moody lord.

In sleep the lady mourned, and the Baron tossed and turned,
　　And oft to himself he said,
"The worms around him creep, and his bloody grave is deep,
　　It cannot give up the dead."

It was near the ringing of matin bell,
　　The night was well-nigh done,
When a heavy sleep on that Baron fell,
　　On the eve of good St. John.

<155>

The lady looked through the chamber fair,
    By the light of a dying flame,
And she was aware of a knight stood there,
    Sir Richard of Coldinghame.

"Alas! away! away!" she cried,
    "For the holy Virgin's sake." —
— "Lady, I know who sleeps by thy side;
    But, lady, he will not awake.

"By Eildon-tree, for long nights three,
    In bloody grave have I lain;
The mass and the death-prayer are said for me,
    But, lady, they're said in vain.

"By the Baron's brand, near Tweed's fair strand,
    Most foully slain I fell,
And my restless sprite on the beacon height
    For a space is doomed to dwell.

"At our trysting-place,[8] for a certain space,
    I must wander to and fro;
But I had not had power to come to thy bower
    Hadst thou not conjured me so." —

Love mastered fear — her brow she crossed;
    — "How, Richard, hast thou sped?
And art thou saved, or art thou lost?" —
    The vision shook his head!

"Who spilleth life, shall forfeit life;
    So bid thy lord believe:
And lawless love is guilt above;
    This awful sign receive."

---

[8] *Trysting-place*, Scottish for place of rendezvous. —WS

<156>

He laid his left hand on an oaken stand,
    His right hand on her arm:
The lady shrunk, and fainting sunk,
    For the touch was fiery warm.

The sable score of fingers four
    Remain on that board impressed,
And for evermore that lady wore
    A covering on her wrist.

There is a nun in Melrose bower
    Ne'er looks upon the sun;
There is a monk in Dryburgh tower,
    He speaketh word to none.

That nun who ne'er beholds the day,
    That monk who speaks to none,
That nun was Smaylho'me's lady gay,
    That monk the bold Baron.

<157>

frederick and Alice

German. — WALTER SCOTT

This ballad is translated (but with such alterations and additions, that it may almost be called original) from the fragment of a Romance, sung in Goethe's Opera of Claudine von Villa Bella.[1]

Frederick leaves the land of France,
  Homewards hastes his steps to measure;
Careless casts the parting glance
  On the scene of former pleasure;

Joying in his prancing steed,
  Keen to prove his untried blade,
Hope's gay dreams the soldier lead
  Over mountain, moor, and glade.

Helpless, ruined, left forlorn,
  Lovely Alice wept alone;
Mourned o'er love's fond contract torn,
  Hope, and peace, and honour flown.

Mark her breast's convulsive throbs!
  See, the tear of anguish flows!
Mingling soon with bursting sobs,
  Loud the laugh of frenzy rose.

Wild she cursed, and wild she prayed;
  Seven long days and nights are o'er;
Death in pity brought his aid,
  As the village bell struck four.

---

[1] *Claudine von Villa Bella* was a Schauspiel or Ballad Opera with a libretto by Goethe, written in 1776. It was set to music by Johann Friedrich Reichard in 1789.

<158>

Far from her, and far from France,
    Faithless Frederick onward rides,
Marking blithe the morning's glance
    Mantling o'er the mountain's sides.

Heard ye not the boding sound,
    As the tongue of yonder tower
Slowly, to the hills around,
    Told the fourth, the fated hour?

Starts the steed, and snuffs the air,
    Yet no cause of dread appears;
Bristles high the rider's hair,
    Struck with strange mysterious fears.

Desperate, as his terrors rise,
    In the steed the spur he hides;
From himself in vain he flies;
    Anxious, restless, on he rides.

Seven long days, and seven long nights,
    Wild he wandered, woe the while!
Ceaseless care, and causeless fright,
    Urge his footsteps many a mile.

Dark the seventh sad night descends;
    Rivers swell, and rain-streams pour;
While the deafening thunder lends
    All the terrors of his roar.

Weary, wet, and spent with toil,
    Where his head shall Frederick hide?
Where, but in yon ruined aisle,
    By the lightning's flash descried.

<159>

To the portal dank and low,
　　Fast his steed the wanderer bound;
Down a ruined staircase, slow
　　Next his darkling way he wound.

Long drear vaults before him lie!
　　Glimmering lights are seen to glide
"Blessed Mary, hear my cry!
　　Deign a sinner's steps to guide!"

Often lost their quivering beam,
　　Still the lights move slow before,
Till they rest their ghastly gleam,
　　Right against an iron door.

Thundering voices from within,
　　Mixed with peals of laughter, rose;
As they fell, a solemn strain
　　Lent its wild and wondrous close!

Midst the din, he seemed to hear
　　Voice of friends, by death removed;
Well he knew that solemn air,
　　'Twas the lay that Alice loved.

Hark! for now a solemn knell
　　Four times on the still night broke;
Four times, at its deadened swell,
　　Echoes from the ruins spoke.

As the lengthened clangours die,
　　Slowly opes the iron door!
Straight a banquet met his eye,
　　But a funeral's form it wore!

<160>

Coffins for the seats extend;
  All with black the board was spread,
Girt by parent, brother, friend,
  Long since numbered with the dead!

Alice, in her grave clothes bound,
  Ghastly smiling, points a seat;
All arose with thundering sound:
  All the expected stranger greet.

High their meagre arms they wave,
  Wild their notes of welcome swell;
"Welcome, traitor, to the grave!
  Perjured, bid the light farewell!"

<161>

The Wild Huntsmen

German.   WALTER SCOTT
            [after GOTTFRIED AUGUST BÜRGER]

The tradition of the "Wild Huntsmen" (Die Wilde Jäger) is a
popular superstition, very generally believed by the peasants of
Germany. Whoever wishes for more information respecting these
imaginary Sportsmen, will find his curiosity fully satisfied by
perusing the first Volume of the German Romance of *The
Necromancer (Der Geister-banner)*.[1] The original of this Ballad is by
Bürger[2], author of the well-known "Leonora." —MGL

The Wildgrave[3] winds his bugle horn;
    To horse, to horse, halloo! halloo!
His fiery courser sniffs the morn,
    And thronging serfs their lord pursue.

The eager pack, from couples freed,
    Dash through the bush, the brier, the brake;
While answering hound, and horn, and steed,
    The mountain echoes startling wake.

The beams of God's own hallowed day
    Had painted yonder spire with gold,
And, calling sinful man to pray,
    Loud, long, and deep the bell had toll'd.

---

[1] *The Necromancer: Or, The Tale of the Black Forest. Founded on Facts. Translated
from the German of Lawrence Flammenburg* [pseud.] 1794. London: William Lane.
[2] Gottfried August Bürger (1747-1794), pioneering German romantic poet,
specialized in the poetic ballad based on folk tales. His 1777 masterpiece, "Die
wilde Jäger," is translated as "The Wild Huntsman" or sometimes, as "The
Chase." In some retellings of the legend, the Huntsman is headless, and this
doubtless inspired Washington Irving's 1820 tale, "The Legend of Sleepy
Hollow." Victor Hugo also penned a fine poem, "Le Chasseur Noir," evoking the
figure of the Wild Huntsman, although not recounting his origins—BR.
[3] Wildgrave is a German title, corresponding to the Earl-Warden of a royal forest
—MGL.

<162>

But still the Wildgrave onward rides;
　　Halloo! halloo! and hark again!
When, spurring from opposing sides,
　　Two stranger horsemen join the train.

Who was each stranger, left and right,
　　Well may I guess, but dare not tell;
The right-hand steed was silver white,
　　The left, the swarthy hue of hell.

The right-hand horsemen, young and fair,
　　His smile was like the morn of May;
The left, from eye of tawny glare,
　　Shot midnight lightning's lurid ray.

He waved his huntsman's cap on high,
　　Cried, "Welcome, welcome, noble lord!
What sport can earth, or sea, or sky,
　　To match the princely chase, afford?" —

— "Cease thy loud bugle's clanging knell," —
　　Cried the fair youth with silver voice;
—"And for devotion's choral swell,
　　Exchange the rude unhallow'd noise.

"To-day th' ill-omen'd chase forbear;
　　Yon bell yet summons to the fane:
To-day the warning spirit hear,
　　To-morrow thou may'st mourn in vain." —

—"Away, and sweep the glades along!"
　　The sable hunter hoarse replies;
— "To muttering monks leave matin song,
　　And bells, and books, and mysteries." —

<163>

The Wildgrave spurred his ardent steed,
    And, launching forward with a bound,
— "Who for thy drowsy priestlike rede
    Would leave the jovial horn and hound?

"Hence, if our manly sport offend:
    With pious fools go chant and pray;
Well hast thou spoke, my dark-brown friend, —
    Halloo! Halloo! and hark away!"

The Wildgrave spurred his courser light,
    O'er moss and moor, o'er holt and hill,
And on the left and on the right,
    Each stranger horseman follow'd still.

Up springs, from yonder tangled thorn,
    A stag more white than mountain snow;
And louder rung the Wildgrave's horn —
    — "Hark forward, forward, holla, ho!" —

A heedless wretch has cross'd the way, —
    He gasps the thundering hoofs below;
But, live who can, or die who may,
    Still forward, forward! On they go.

See where yon simple fences meet,
    A field with autumn's blessings crowned;
See, prostrate at the Wildgrave's feet,
    A husbandman with toil embrown'd.

— "Oh, mercy! mercy! noble Lord;
    "Spare the poor's pittance," was his cry;
"Earned by the sweat these brows have pour'd
    In scorching hour of fierce July." —

<164>

Earnest the right-hand stranger pleads,
    The left still cheering to the prey:
The impetuous Earl no warning heeds,
    But furious holds the onward way.

— "Away, thou hound, so basely born,
    Or dread the scourge's echoing blow!" —
Then loudly rung his bugle-horn,
    — "Hark forward, forward, holla, ho!"

So said, so done — a single bound
    Clears the poor labourer's humble pale:
Wild follows man, and horse, and hound,
    Like dark December's stormy gale.

And man, and horse, and hound, and horn,
    Destructive sweep the field along,
While joying o'er the wasted corn
    Fell Famine marks the madd'ning throng.

Again up-roused, the timorous prey
    Scours moss and moor, and holt and hill;
Hard run, he feels his strength decay,
    And trusts for life his simple skill.

Too dangerous solitude appear'd;
    He seeks the shelter of the crowd;
Amid the flock's domestic herd
    His harmless head he hopes to shroud.

O'er moss and moor, and holt and hill,
    His track the steady bloodhounds trace;
O'er moss and moor, unwearied still,
    The furious Earl pursues the chase.

<165>

Full lowly did the herdsman fall:
    —"Oh, spare, thou noble Baron, spare
These herds, a widow's little all;
    These flocks, an orphan's fleecy care." —

Earnest the right-hand stranger pleads,
    The left still cheering to the prey;
The Earl nor prayer nor pity heeds,
    But furious keeps the onward way.

— "Unmannered dog! To stop my sport
    Vain were thy cant and beggar whine,
Though human spirits of thy sort
    "Were tenants of these carrion kine!"

Again he winds his bugle horn,
    — "Hark forward, forward, holla, ho!"
And through the herd in ruthless scorn,
    He cheers his furious hounds to go.

In heaps the throttled victims fall;
    Down sinks their mangled herdsman near;
The murd'rous cries the stag appal,
    Again he starts, new-nerved by fear.

With blood besmeared, and white with foam,
    While big the tears of anguish pour,
He seeks, amid the forest's gloom,
    The humble hermit's hallowed bow'r.

But man and horse, and horn and hound,
    Fast rattling on his traces go;
The sacred chapel rung around
    With hark away, and holla, ho!

<166>

All mild, amid the route profane,
    The holy hermit pour'd his prayer:
— "Forbear with blood God's house to stain;
    Revere His altar, and forbear!

"The meanest brute has rights to plead,
    Which, wrong'd by cruelty, or pride,
Draw vengeance on the ruthless head;
    Be warned at length, and turn aside." —

Still the fair horseman anxious pleads,
    The black, wild whooping, points the prey;
Alas! the Earl no warning heeds,
    But frantic keeps the forward way.

— "Holy or not, or right or wrong,
    Thy altar and its rites I spurn;
Not sainted martyrs' sacred song,
    Not God himself, shall make me turn." —

He spurs his horse, he winds his horn,
    — "Hark forward, forward, holla, ho!"
But off, on whirlwind's pinions borne,
    The stag, the hut, the hermit, go.

And horse and man, and horn and hound,
    And clamour of the chase was gone:
For hoofs and howls, and bugle sound,
    A deadly silence reign'd alone.

Wild gazed the affrighted Earl around; —
    He strove in vain to wake his horn,
In vain to call; for not a sound
    Could from his anxious lips be borne.

<167>

He listens for his trusty hounds;
    No distant baying reached his ears;
His courser, rooted to the ground,
    The quickening spur unmindful bears.

Still dark and darker frown the shades,
    Dark as the darkness of the grave;
And not a sound the still invades,
    Save what a distant torrent gave.

High o'er the sinner's humbled head
    At length the solemn silence broke;
And from a cloud of swarthy red,
    The awful voice of thunder spoke:

— "Oppressor of creation fair!
    Apostate spirit's harden'd tool!
Scorner of God! scourge of the poor!
    The measure of thy cup is full.

"Be chased for ever through the wood,
    For ever roam the affrighted wild;
And let thy fate instruct the proud,
    God's meanest creature is His child." —

'Twas hushed: one flash of sombre glare
    With yellow tinged the forest's brown;
Up rose the Wildgrave's bristling hair,
    And horror chilled each nerve and bone.

Cold poured the sweat in freezing rill;
    A rising wind began to sing;
And louder, louder, louder still,
    Brought storm and tempest on its wing.

<168>

Earth heard the call — her entrails rend;
    From yawning rifts, with many a yell,
Mixed with sulphureous flames, ascend
    The misbegotten dogs of hell.

What ghastly huntsman next arose,
    Well may I guess, but dare not tell:
His eye like midnight lightning glows,
    His steed the swarthy hue of hell.

The Wildgrave flies o'er bush and thorn,
    With many a shriek of helpless woe:
Behind him hound, and horse, and horn,
    And hark away, and holla, ho!

With wild despair's reverted eye,
    Close, close behind, he marks the throng;
With bloody fangs, and eager cry,
    In frantic fear he scours along.

Still, still shall last the dreadful chase,
    Till time itself shall have an end;
By day, they scour earth's caverned space,
    At midnight's witching hour, ascend.

This is the horn, and hound, and horse,
    That oft the lated peasant hears:
Appall'd, he signs the frequent cross,
    When the wild din invades his ears.

The wakeful priest oft drops a tear
    For human pride, for human woe,
When at his midnight mass, he hears
    The infernal cry of holla, ho!

<169>

WALTER SCOTT ON
"THE WILD HUNTSMAN"

This is a translation, or rather an imitation, of the *Wilde Jäger* of the German poet Bürger. The tradition upon which it is founded bears, that formerly a Waldgrave, or keeper of a royal forest, named Faulkenburg, was so much addicted to the pleasures of the chase, and otherwise so extremely profligate and cruel, that he not only followed this unhallowed amusement on the Sabbath, and other days consecrated to religious duty, but accompanied it with the most unheard-of oppression of the poor peasants, who were under his vassalage. When this second Nimrod died, the people adopted a superstition, founded probably on the various uncouth sounds heard in the depth of a German forest, during the silence of the night. They conceived they still heard the cry of the Waldgrave's hounds; and the well-known cheer of the deceased hunter, the sounds of his horses' feet, and the rustling of the branches before the game, the pack, and the sportsmen, are also distinctly discriminated; but the phantoms are rarely, if ever, visible.

Once, as a benighted *Chasseur* heard this infernal chase pass by him, at the sound of the halloo, with which the Spectre Huntsman cheered his hounds, he could not refrain from crying, 'Gluck zu Falkenburgh!' [Good sport to ye, Falkenburgh!] 'Dost thou wish me good sport?' answered a hoarse voice; 'thou shalt share the game;' and there was thrown at him what seemed to be a huge piece of foul carrion. The daring Chasseur lost two of his best horses soon after, and never perfectly recovered the personal effects of this ghostly greeting. This tale, though told with some variations, is universally believed all over Germany.

The French had a similar tradition concerning an aerial hunter who infested the forest of Fontainebleau. He was sometimes visible; when he appeared as a huntsman, surrounded with dogs, a tall grisly figure. Some account of him may be found in 'Sully's Memoirs,' who says he was called *Le Grand Veneur*. At one time he chose to hunt so near the palace, that the attendants, and, if I mistake not, Sully himself, came out into the court, supposing it was the sound of the king returning from the chase. This phantom is elsewhere called St. Hubert.

The superstition seems to have been very general, as appears from the following fine poetical description of this phantom chase, as it was heard in the wilds of Ross-shire:

<170>

'Ere since of old, the haughty thanes of Ross, —
So to the simple swain tradition tells —
Were wont with clans, and ready vassals throng'd,
To wake the bounding stag, or guilty wolf,
There oft is heard, at midnight, or at noon,
Beginning faint, but rising still more loud,
And nearer, voice of hunters, and of hounds,
And horns, hoarse winded, blowing far and keen:—
Forthwith the hubbub multiplies; the gale
Labors with wilder shrieks, and rifer din
Of hot pursuit; the broken cry of deer
Mangled by throttling dogs; the shouts of men,
And hoofs, thick beating on the hollow hill.
Sudden the grazing heifer in the vale
Starts at the noise, and both the herdsman's ears
Tingle with inward dread. Aghast, he eyes
The mountain's height, and all the ridges round,
Yet not one trace of living wight discerns,
Nor knows, o'erawed, and trembling as he stands,
To what, or whom, he owes his idle fear,
To ghost, to witch, to fairy, or to fiend;
But wonders, and no end of wondering finds.
   Albania — reprinted in *Scottish Descriptive Poems*, pp. 167-168.[4]

A posthumous miracle of Father Lesley, a Scottish capuchin, related
to his being buried on a hill haunted by these unearthly cries of hounds
and huntsmen. After his sainted relics had been deposited there, the noise
was never heard more. The reader will find this, and other miracles,
recorded in the life of Father Bonaventura[5], which is written in the choicest
Italian. —(Scott, *Poems* 653)

---

[4] *Scottish Descriptive Poems*, a collection by John Leyden, published in
Edinburgh in 1803.
[5] *Father Bonaventura*. Baron Bonaventura (1610-1696) was an Irish Franciscan
theologian and historian who traveled extensively through Italy and Germany.

<171>

The Old Woman of Berkeley[1]

ROBERT SOUTHEY

The raven croak'd as she sate at her meal,
    And the Old Woman knew what he said,
And she grew pale at the raven's tale,
    And sicken'd, and went to her bed.

— "Now fetch me my children, and fetch them with speed,"
    The Old Woman of Berkeley said,
— "The monk my son, and my daughter the nun;
    Bid them hasten, or I shall be dead."

The monk her son, and her daughter the nun,
    Their way to Berkeley went,
And they have brought, with pious thought,
    The holy sacrament.

The Old Woman shriek'd as they enter'd her door,
    'Twas fearful her shrieks to hear;
— "Now take the sacrament away,
    For mercy, my children dear!"

Her lip it trembled with agony,
    The sweat ran down her brow,
— "I have tortures in store for evermore,
    Oh! spare me, my children, now!" —

Away they sent the sacrament;
    The fit it left her weak;
She look'd at her children with ghastly eyes,
    And faintly struggled to speak.

---

[1] This poem in *Southey's Poems*, Vol. III ("comprising Vols V and VI"), with the following subtitle: "A Ballad, / Showing How an Old Woman Rode Double/ And Who Rode Before Her." ("Rode double" means two on a horse.) Southey dates the poem to Hereford, 1798.

<172>

— "All kind of sin I have rioted in,
　　And the judgment now must be;
But I secured my childrens' souls,
　　Oh! pray my children, for me!

"I have suck'd the breath of sleeping babes,
　　The fiends have been my slaves:
I have 'nointed myself with infants' fat,
　　And feasted on rifled graves.

"And the Fiend will fetch me now in fire,
　　My witchcrafts to atone;
And I, who have rifled the dead man's grave,
　　Shall never have rest in my own.

"Bless, I intreat, my winding sheet,
　　My children, I beg of you!
And with holy water sprinkle my shroud,
　　And sprinkle my coffin too.

"And let me be chain'd in my coffin of stone,
　　And fasten it strong, I implore,
With iron bars; and let it be chain'd
　　With three chains to the church floor.

"And bless the chains, and sprinkle them;
　　And let fifty priests stand round;
Who night and day the mass may say
　　Where I lie on the ground.

"And let fifty choristers be there,
　　The funeral dirge to sing,
Who day, and night, by the tapers' light,
　　Their aid to me may bring.

<173>

"Let the church bells all, both great and small,
    Be toll'd by night and day,
To drive from thence the fiends who come
    To bear my corpse away.

"And ever have the church door barr'd
    After the even song;
And I beseech you, children dear,
    Let the bars and bolts be strong.

"And let this be three days and nights,
    My Wretched corpse to save;
Preserve me so long from the fiendish throng,
    And then I may rest in my grave." —

The Old Woman of Berkeley laid her down,
    And her eyes grew deadly dim;
Short came her breath, and the struggle of death
    Did loosen every limb.

They bless'd the Old Woman's winding sheet
    With rites and prayers as due;
With holy water they sprinkled her shroud,
    And they sprinkled her coffin too.

And they chain'd her in a coffin of stone,
    And with iron barr'd it down;
And in the church, with three strong chains,
    They chain'd it to the ground.

And they bless'd the chains, and sprinkled them,
    And fifty priests stood round,
By night and day the mass to say
    Where she lay on the ground.

<174>

And fifty choristers were there
　　To sing the funeral song,
And a hallow'd taper blaz'd in the hand
　　Of all the sacred throng.

To see the priests and choristers
　　It was a goodly sight,
Each holding, as it were a staff,
　　A taper burning bright.

And the church bells all, both great and small,
　　Did toll so loud and long,
And they have barr'd the church door hard.
　　After the even song.

And the first night the tapers' light
　　Burnt steadily and clear;
But they without a hideous rout
　　Of angry fiends could hear;

A hideous roar at the church door,
　　Like a long thunder peal,
And the priests they pray'd, and the choristers sung,
　　Louder in fearful zeal.

Loud toll'd the bell, the priests pray'd well,
　　The tapers they burnt bright;
The monk her son, and her daughter the nun,
　　They told their beads all night.

The cock he crew, away then flew
　　The fiends from the herald of day,
And undisturb'd the choristers sing,
　　And the fifty priests they pray.

<175>

The second night the tapers' light
   Burnt dismally and blue,
And every one saw his neighbour's face
   Like a dead man's face to view.

And yells and cries without arise,
   That the stoutest heart might shock;
And a deafening roaring, like a cataract pouring
   Over a mountain rock.

The monk and the nun they told their beads
   As fast as they could tell;
And aye, as louder grew the noise,
   The faster went the bell.

Louder and louder the choristers sung,
   As they trembled more and more;
And the fifty priests pray'd to heaven for aid;
   They never had pray'd so before.

The cock he crew, away then flew
   The fiends from the herald of day;
And undisturb'd the choristers sing,
   And the fifty priests they pray.

The third night came, and the tapers' flame
   A hideous stench did make;
And they burnt as though they had been dipp'd
   In the burning brimstone lake.

And the loud commotion, like the rushing of ocean,
   Grew momently more and more,
And strokes, as of a battering ram,
   Did shake the strong church door.

<176>

The bellmen they, for very fear,
    Could toll the bell no longer;
And still, as louder grew the strokes,
    Their fear it grew the stronger.

The monk and nun forgot their beads,
    They fell on the ground dismay'd;
There was not a single saint in heaven
    Whom they did not call to aid.

And the choristers' song, that late was so strong,
    Grew a quaver of consternation,
For the church did rock, as an earthquake shock
    Uplifted its foundation.

And a sound was heard like the trumpet's blast,
    That shall one day wake the dead;
The strong church door could bear no more,
    And the bolts and bars they fled.

And the tapers' light was extinguish'd quite,
    And the choristers faintly sung,
And the priests, dismay'd, panted and pray'd,
    Till fear froze every tongue.

And in he came, with eyes of flame,
    The Fiend to fetch the dead,
And all the church with his presence glow'd
    Like a fiery furnace red.

He laid his hand on the iron chains,
    And like flax they moulder'd asunder;
And the coffin lid, that was barr'd so firm,
    He burst with his voice of thunder.

<177>

The Witch of Berkeley carried off by the Devil.
From Olaus Magnus, *Historia de Gentibus Septentrionalibus*, 1555.

And he bade the Old Woman of Berkeley rise,
    And come with her master away;
And the cold sweat stood on the cold cold corpse,
    At the voice she was forced to obey.

She rose on her feet in her winding sheet,
    Her dead flesh quiver'd with fear,
And a groan like that which the Old Woman gave
    Never did mortal hear.

She follow'd the Fiend to the church door,
    There stood a black horse there,
His breath was red like furnace smoke,
    His eyes like a meteor's glare.

The fiendish force flung her on the horse,
    And he leap'd up before,
And away like the lightning's speed they went,
    And she was seen no more.

They saw her no more, but her cries and shrieks
    For four miles round they could hear,
And children at rest at their mothers' breast,
    Started and scream'd with fear.

<178>

THE ORIGINAL LATIN VERSION OF THE STORY
Attrib. **Matthew of Westminster**

A. D. 852. Circa dies istos, mulier quaedam malefica, in villá quae Berkeleia dicitur degens, gulae amatrix ac petulantiae, flagitiis modum usque in senium et auguriis non ponens, usque ad mortem impudica permansit. Haec die quadam cum sederet ad prandium, cornicula quam pro delitüs pascebat, nescio quid garrire coepit; quo audito, mulieris cultellus de manu excidit, simul et facies pallescere coepit, et emisso rugitu, Hodie, inquit, accipiam grande incommodum, hodieque ad sulcum ultimum meum pervenit aratrum. Quo dicto, nuncius doloris intravit; muliere vero percunctata ad quid veniret, Affero, inquit, tibi filii tui obitum et totius familiae ejus ex subitá ruiná interitum. Hoc quoque dolore mulier permota, lecto protinus decubuit graviter infirmata; sentiensque morbum subrepere ad vitalia, liberos quos habuit superstites, monachum, videlicet, et monacham, per epistolam invitavit; advenientes autem voce singultiente alloquitur. Ego, inquit, o pueri, meo miserabili fato daemoniacis semper artibus inservivi; ego omnium vitiorum sentina, ego illecebrarum omnium fui magistra. Erat tamen mihi inter haec mala, spes vestrae religionis, quae meam solidaret animam desperatam; vos expectabam propugnatores contra daemones, tutores contra saevissimos hostes. Nunc igitur quoniam ad finem vitae perveni, rogo vos per materna ubera, ut mea tentatis alleviare tormenta. Inserite me defunctam in corio cervino, ac deinde in sarcophago lapideo supponite, operculumque ferro et plumbo constringite, ac demim lapidem tribus cathenis ferreis et fortissimis circumdantes, clericos quinquaginta psalmorum cantores, et tot per tres dies presbyteros missarum celebratores applicate, qui feroces lenigent adversariorum incursus. Ita si tribus noctibus secura jacucro quarta die me infodite humo.

Factumqite est ut praeceperat illis. Sed, proh dolor! nil preces, nil lacrymae, nil demum valuere cathenae. Primis enim duabus noctibus, cum chori psallentium corpori assistabant, advenientes Daemones ostium ecclesiae confregerunt ingenti obice clausum, extremasque cathenas negotio levi dirumpunt: media atem, quea fortior erat, illibata manebat. Tertiá autem nocte, circa gallicinium, strepitu hostium adventantium, omne monasterium visum est a fundamento moveri. Unus ergo daemonum, et vultu caeteris terribilior, et staturá eminentior, januas ecclesiae impetu violento concussas in fragmenta dejecit.

Divexerunt clerici cum laicis, metu steterunt omnium capilli, et psalmorum concentus defecit. Daemon ergo gestu ut videbatur arroganti ad sepulchrum accedens, et nomen mulieris modicum ingeminans, surgere imperavit. Quá respondente, quod nequiret pro vinculis, Jam malo tuo,

<179>

inquit, solveris; et protinus cathenam quae caeterorum ferocium daemonium deluserat, velut stuppeum vinculum rumpebat. Operculum etiam sepulchri pede depellens, mulierem palam omnibus ab ecclesiá extraxit, ubi prae foribus niger equus superbe hinniens videbatur, uncis ferreis et clavis undique confixus, super quem misera mulier projecta, ab oculis assistentium evanuit. Audiebantur tamen clamores, per quatuor fere miliaria, horribiles, auxilium postulantes.

Ista itaque qua retuli incredibilia non erunt, si legatur beati Gregorii dialogus, in quo refert, hominem in ecclesiá sepultum, a daemonibus foras ejectum. Et apud Francos, Carolus Martellus insignis vir fortitudinis, qui Saracenos Gallium ingressos, Hispaniam redire compulit, exactis vitae suae diebus, in Ecclesiá beati Dionysii legitur fuisse sepultus. Sed quia patrimonia, cum decimis omnium fere ecclesiarum Galliae, pro stipendio commilitonum suorum mutilaverat, miserabiliter a malignis spiritibus de sepulchro corporaliter avulsus, usque in hodiernum diem nusquam comparuit.[2]

---

[2] Southey adds the following note: "The story is also related by Olaus Magnus, and in the *Nuremberg Chronicle*. But William of Malmesbury seems to have been the original authority, and he had the story from an eye-witness. 'When I shall have related it,' he says, 'the credit of the narrative will not be shaken, though the minds of the hearers should be incredulous, for I have heard it from a man of such character *who would swear he had seen it*, that I should blush to disbelieve' " (Sharpe's *William of Malmesbury*, p. 264).
Southey may be mistaken here. The Latin version the poet found in the cathedral library was a chronicle entry for the year 845 CE; the narration in William of Malmesbury's *Chronicle*, however, is an entry in a section for the years 1042-1066. (Giles edition 1904, pp. 230-232). Only by comparing the Latin of both versions would we know whether one monk copied the narrative from another, or whether each is distinct in details and language. In any event, Malmesbury's assertion that this fable had to be true, because he heard it from an honest man, is hilarious. Who inserted what in the record, and when, and whether the tale was back-dated, remains a mystery —BR.

<180>

OF A CERTAIN WITCH,
AND HER MISERABLE DEATH[3]

In those days there lived in the village of Berkeley a certain woman, who was a witch, a lover of her belly, and given to lasciviousness, forsaking not her flagitious courses and her fortune-telling even in her old age, but remaining shameless even to her death. One day, as she sat at dinner a young raven, which she kept for her amusement, began to chatter I know not what; on which the woman let the knife drop from her hand, and turning pale in the face, began to cry, and exclaimed, "I shall hear of some heavy calamity today, for my plough is come to-day to the last furrow;" and no sooner had she so said, than there entered a messenger with doleful tidings. On her inquiring why he came, he replied, "I have to inform you that your son and all his family have been suddenly crushed to death." Struck with this sorrowful news, the woman immediately became very ill and took to her bed; and sensible that the disease was creeping on to her vitals, she sent a letter for her yet surviving children, the one a monk and the other a nun. On their arrival she addressed them with sobs after this manner, "My children, it has been my miserable fate, that I have all my life given myself to devilish practices, having been the sink of every vice, and the teacher of all manner of impurities. Yet, in the midst of my wickednesses, I placed my hope for the salvation of my perishing soul in your religion, trusting that you would be my defence against my adversaries, my guardians against my cruel foes. Now, therefore, that I am come to the end of my life, I beseech you by these breasts which have nourished you, that you do your endeavours to alleviate my torments. As soon as I am dead, sew me up in a deer-skin, and then place me in a stone coffin, fastening well the lid with iron and lead, and binding it round with three very strong iron chains; after which, procure fifty ecclesiastics to sing psalms, and as many priests to celebrate masses for three days, that so the fierce attacks of my enemies may be repelled; and then, if I shall lie in security for three nights, on the fourth day bury me under ground." They did as she had directed; but, alas! neither prayers, nor tears, nor chains availed anything; for on the first two nights, while the quires were singing around the corpse, the devils came and burst open the church door, which was fastened with a huge bar, and broke with ease the chains that were about the extremities of the coffin; but the middle one was too strong for them, and remained entire. But on the third night, about cock-crowing, the whole of the monastery seemed to be shaken from its foundation by

---

[3] Roger of Wendover, *Flowers of History (Flores Historiarum)*, (previously attributed to Matthew Paris, also known as Matthew of Westminster). J.A. Giles, trans. (1849). This book is a Latin chronicle of English history, compiled by a succession of monks, and ending in 1326 CE.

<181>

the noise of the approaching demons. One of the devils, who was more terrible in look and taller of stature than the rest, with a violent onset shivered the church-doors to fragments; the clergy and laity became stiff with fear, and their hair stood on end, and the singing of the psalms ceased. Then the demon, approaching the tomb with a haughty air, called the woman by her name which has not been recorded, and commanded her to rise; she replied that she could not for the fastenings. "There is now no hindrance," said he, and straightway he broke the chain which had baffled the efforts of the other devils, with as much ease as if it had been of tow; and then kicking off the lid of the coffin, he in the face of all dragged the woman forth from the church, where was seen before the doors a black steed, proudly neighing, with hoofs of iron, and completely caparisoned, upon which the wretched woman was thrown, and she quickly disappeared from the sight of the beholders; yet her fearful shrieks were heard for nearly four miles as she cried loudly for help. Now what I have related will not be considered incredible, if you read the dialogue of the blessed pope Gregory, where he narrates how a man, who had been buried in a church, was dragged out of it by devils; and among the Franks, Charles Martel, a man of singular courage, who compelled the Saracens who had entered Gaul to retire back into Spain, after he had ended his days, was buried, as it is said, in the church of the blessed Dionysius; but because he had invaded the patrimony of nearly all the churches of Gaul by applying the tithes to the payment of his soldiers, his body was miserably torn from the tomb by malignant spirits, and was never more seen unto this day.

<182>

ROBERT SOUTHEY ON THE ORIGINS
OF "THE OLD WOMAN OF BERKELEY"

My late friend, Mr. William Taylor of Norwich, whom none who knew him intimately can ever call to mind without affection and regret, has this passage in his Life of Dr. Sayers, "Not long after this (the year 1800), Mr. Robert Southey visited Norwich, was introduced to Dr. Sayers, and partook those feelings of complacent admiration which his presence was adapted to inspire. — Dr. Sayers pointed out to us in conversation, as adapted for the theme of a ballad, a story related by Olaus Magnus of a witch, whose coffin was confined by three chains, sprinkled with holy water; but who was, nevertheless, carried off by demons. Already, I believe, Dr. Sayers had made a ballad on the subject, so did I, and so did Mr. Southey; but after seeing the Old Woman of Berkeley, we agreed in awarding to it the preference. Still, the very different manner in which each had employed the same basis of narration might render welcome the opportunity of comparison; but I have not found among the papers of Dr. Sayers a copy of his poem."

There is a mistake here as to the date. This, my first visit to Norwich, was in the spring of 1798; and I had so much to interest me there I in the society of my kind host and friend, Mr. William Taylor, that the mention at Dr. Sayers' table of the story in Olaus Magnus made no impression on me at the time, and was presently forgotten. Indeed, if I had known that either he or his friend had written or intended to write a ballad upon the subject, that knowledge, however much the story might have pleased me, would have withheld me from all thought of versifying it. In the autumn of the same year, I passed some days at Hereford with Mr. William Bowyer Thomas, one of the friends with whom, in 1796, I had visited the Arrabida Convent near Setubal. By his means I obtained permission to make use of the books in the Cathedral Library, and accordingly I was locked up for several mornings in that part of the Cathedral where the books were kept in chains. So little were these books used at that time, that in placing them upon the shelves, no regard had been had to the length of the chains; and when the volume which I wished to consult was fastened to one of the upper shelves by a short chain, the only means by which it was possible to make use of it was, by piling upon the reading desk as many volumes with longer chains as would reach up to the length of its tether; then, by standing on a chair, I was able to effect my purpose.

<183>

There, and thus, I first read the story of the Old Woman of Berkeley, in Matthew of Westminster,[4] and transcribed it into a pocket-book. I had no recollection of what had passed at Dr. Sayers's; but the circumstantial details in the monkish Chronicle impressed me so strongly, that I began to versify them that very evening. It was the last day of our pleasant visit at Hereford; and on the following morning the remainder of the Ballad was pencilled in post-chaise on our way to Abberley.

Mr. Wathen, a singular and obliging person, who afterwards made a voyage to the East Indies, and published an account of what he saw there, traced for me a facsimile of a wooden cut in the *Nuremberg Chronicle* (which was among the prisoners in the Cathedral). It represents the Old Woman's forcible abduction from her intended place of burial. This was put into the hands of a Bristol artist; and the engraving in wood which he made from it was prefixed to the Ballad when first published in the second volume of my poems, 1799. The Devil alludes to it in his Walk [another famous Southey poem, "The Devil's Walk"], when he complains of a certain poet as having "put him in ugly ballads with libellous pictures for sale."

The passage from Matthew of Westminster was prefixed to the Ballad when first published, and it has continued to be so in every subsequent edition of my minor poems from that time to the present: for whenever I have founded either a poem, or part of one, upon any legend, or portion of history, I have either extracted the passage to which I was indebted, if its length allowed, or have referred to it.

Mr. Payne Collier, however, after the Ballad, with its parentage affixed, had been twenty years before the public, discovered that I had copied the story from Heywood's *Nine Books of Various History concerning Women*, and that I had not thought proper to acknowledge the obligation. The discovery is thus stated in that gentleman's *Poetical Decameron* (vol. i. p. 323). Speaking of the book, one of his Interlocutors says, "It is not of such rarity or singularity as to deserve particular notice now; only if you refer to p. 443, you will find the story on which Mr. Southey founded his mock-ballad of the Old Woman of Berkeley. You will see, too, that the mode in which it is told is extremely similar.

MORTON. Had Mr. Southey seen Heywood's book?

BOURNE. It is not improbable; or some quotation from it, the resemblance is so exact; you may judge from the few following sentences.

Part of Heywood's narration is then given, upon which one of the speakers observes, "The resemblance is exact, and it is not unlikely that Heywood and Southey copied from the same original."

---

[4] *Matthew of Westminster*, also known as Matthew Paris, was then attributed as the principal author of the chronicle. The principal compiler is now believed to be Roger of Wendover. The Giles translation cited here is thus the same Latin text—BR.

<184>

BOURNE. Perhaps so: Heywood quotes *Guillerimus*,[5] in *Special. Histor.*, *lib. xxvi c.26*. He afterwards relates, as Southey, that the Devil placed the Old Woman of Berkeley before him on a black horse, and that her screams were heard four miles off.[6]

It cannot, however, be disputed, that Mr. Payne Collier has made one discovery relating to this subject; for he has discovered that the Old Woman of Berkeley is a mock-ballad. Certainly this was never suspected by the Author, or any of his friends. It obtained a very different character in Russia, where having been translated and published, it was prohibited for this singular reason, that children were said to be frightened by it. This I was told by a Russian traveller who called upon me at Keswick.

—Keswick, March 8, 1838.

---

[5] *Guillerimus.* Latin for William, which brings us back again, most likely, to William of Malmesbury —BR.
[6] *Four miles off.* This is from the Latin original which Southey always attached to the poem: *Audiebantur tamen clamores, per quatuor fere miliaria* [the sound carried past four mile-stones], *horribiles, auxilium postulantes* —BR.

<185>

Bishop Bruno

ROBERT SOUTHEY

Bruno, the Bishop of Herbipolitanum, sailing in the river of
Danubius with Henry III, then emperor, being not far from a place
which the Germanes call Ben Strudel, or the devouring gulfe, which
is neere unto Grinon, a castle in Austria, a spirit was heard
clamouring aloud, 'Ho, ho, Bishop Bruno! whither art thou
travelling? But, dispose of thyselfe how thou pleaseth, thou shalt be
my prey and spoil.' At the hearing of these words, they were all
stupefied; and the bishop, with the rest, crost and blessed
themselves. The issue was, that within a short time after, the bishop
feasting with the emperor in a castle belonging to the Countess of
Esburch, a rafter fell from the roof of the chamber wherein they sate,
and strooke him dead at the table. — Heywood's *Hierarchies of the
Blessed Angels*.[1]

Bishop Bruno[2] awoke in the dead midnight,
And he heard his heart beat loud with affright;
He dreamt he had rung the palace bell,
And the sound it gave was his passing knell.

Bishop Bruno smiled at his fears so vain,
He turn'd to sleep, and he dreamt again;
He rung at the palace gate once more,
And Death was the porter that open'd the door.

He started up at the fearful dream,
And he heard at his window the screech-owl scream;
Bishop Bruno slept no more that night,
O glad was he when he saw the day-light.

---

[1] This prefatory note was always affixed to the poem in Southey's own editions.
Lewis omitted it. Thomas Heywood (c. 1570-1641) wrote *Hierarchies of the Blessed
Angels*, in 1635.
[2] Bishop Bruno was the son of Henry II, Duke of Bavaria and brother of Henry
II of Bavaria (Holy Roman Emperor and later, Saint Henry). Bruno was Bishop
of Augsburg, Germany, circa 1006 until his death in 1029.

<186>

Now forth he goes in proud array,
For he with the Emperor dines to-day;
There was not a baron in Germany,
That went with a nobler train than he.

Before and behind his soldiers ride,
The people throng'd to see the pride;
They bow'd the head, and the knee they bent,
But nobody bless'd him as he went.

He went so stately and so proud,
When he heard a voice that cried aloud —
— "Ho! ho! Bishop Bruno! you travel with glee,
But know, Bishop Bruno, you travel to me." —

Behind, and before, and on either side,
He look'd, but nobody he espied;
And the Bishop he grew cold with fear,
For he heard the words distinct and clear.

And when he rung at the palace bell,
He almost expected to hear his knell;
And when the porter turn'd the key,
He almost expected Death to see.

But soon the Bishop recover'd his glee,
For the Emperor welcom'd him royally;
And now the tables were spread, and there
Were choicest wines, and dainty fare.

And now the Bishop had bless'd the meat,
When, a voice was heard, as he sat in his seat;
— "With the Emperor now you are dining in glee,
But know, Bishop Bruno, you sup with me." —

<187>

The Bishop then grew pale with affright,
And instantly lost his appetite;
And all the wine and dainty cheer
Could not comfort his heart so sick with fear.

But by little and little recover'd he,
For the wine went flowing merrily,
And he forgot his former dread,
And his cheeks again grew rosy red.

When he sat down to the royal fare,
Bishop Bruno was the saddest man there;
But when the maskers entered the hall,
He was the merriest man of all.

Then from amid the maskers' crowd
There went a voice hollow and loud;
"You have pass'd the day, Bishop Bruno, with glee,
But you must pass the night with me!"

His cheek grows pale, and his eye-balls glare,
And stiff round his tonsure rises his hair:
With that there came one from the maskers' band,
And he took the Bishop by the hand.

The bony hand suspended his breath,
His marrow grew cold at the touch of Death;
On saints in vain he attempted to call —
Bishop Bruno fell dead in the palace hall.

[*1798*]

<188>

Lord William

ROBERT SOUTHEY

No eye beheld when William plunged
    Young Edmund in the stream;
No human ear but William's heard
    Young Edmund's drowning scream.

Submissive all the Vassals own'd
    The murderer for their Lord,
And he, the rightful heir, possess'd
    The house of Erlingford.[1]

The ancient house of Erlingford
    Stood 'midst a fair domain,
And Severn's[2] ample waters near
    Roll'd through the fertile plain.

And often the way-faring man
    Would love to linger there,
Forgetful of his onward road,
    To gaze on scenes so fair.

But never could Lord William dare
    To gaze on Severn's stream;
In every wind that swept its waves
    He heard young Edmund scream.

---

[1] Although there is a town of Erlingford in County Kilkenny in Ireland, there does not appear to be a town or seat of that name in Britain. The name may be fanciful and its etymology is apt to the story: "Erling" means "heir to a clan chief" and "ford" is a river crossing.

[2] The use of the Severn clouds the likelihood of fixing a locale for this poem, since the Severn is the longest river in Britain, running through both England and Wales. The reference to "tide," however, would place us at the river below Gloucester, where the waters are affected by tides, and the water level in the tidal basin rises and falls by as much as 48 feet, the world's largest tidal range.

<189>

In vain at midnight's silent hour
    Sleep closed the murderer's eyes;
In every dream the murderer saw
    Young Edmund's form arise.

In vain, by restless conscience driven,
    Lord William left his home,
Far from the scenes that saw his guilt,
    In pilgrimage to roam.

To other climes the pilgrim fled,
    But could not fly despair;
He sought his home again, but peace
    Was still a stranger there.

Each hour was tedious long, yet swift
    The months appear'd to roll;
And now the day return'd that shook
    With terror William's soul.

A day that William never felt
    Return without dismay.
For well had conscience kalender'd
    Young Edmund's dying day.

A fearful day was that! the rains
    Fell fast, with tempest roar,
And the swoln tide of Severn spread
    Far on the level shore.

In vain Lord William sought the feast,
    In vain he quaff'd the bowl,
And strove with noisy mirth to drown
    The anguish of his soul.

<190>

The tempest, as its sudden swell
    In gusty howlings came,
With cold arid death-like feelings seem'd
    To thrill his shuddering frame.

Reluctant now, as night came on,
    His lonely couch he press'd;
And, wearied out, he sunk to sleep,
    To sleep, but not to rest.

Beside that couch his brother's form,
    Lord Edmund, seem'd to stand,
Such and so pale as when in death
    He grasp'd his brother's hand

Such and so pale his face as when,
    With faint and faltering tongue,
To William's care, a dying charge,
    He left his orphan son.

— "I bade thee, with a father's love,
    My orphan Edmund guard;
Well, William, hast thou kept thy charge!
    Now take thy due reward." —

He started up, each limb convuls'd
    With agonizing fear;
He only heard the storm of night —
    'Twas music to his ear.

When lo! the voice of loud alarm
    His inmost soul appals,
— "What ho! Lord William, rise in haste!
    The water saps thy walls!" —

<191>

He rose in haste: beneath the walls
    He saw the flood appear;
It hemm'd him round, 'twas midnight now,
    No human aid was near.

He heard the shout of joy, for now
    A boat approach'd the wall,
And, eager to the welcome aid,
    They crowd for safety all.

— "My boat is small," the boatman cried,
    "This dangerous haste forbear!
Wait other aid; this little bark
    But one from hence can bear." —

Lord William leap'd into the boat,
    "Haste — haste to yonder shore!
And ample wealth shall well reward,
    Ply swift and strong the oar." —

The boatman plied the oar, the boat
    Went light along the stream;
Sudden Lord William heard a cry
    Like Edmund's drowning scream.

The boatman paus'd, — "Methought I heard
    A child's distressful cry!" —
" 'Twas but the howling wind of night,"
    Lord William made reply.

"Haste, haste — ply swift and strong the oar!
    Haste — haste across the stream!" —
Again Lord William heard a cry
    Like Edmund's drowning scream.

<192>

— "I heard a child's distressful scream," —
 The boatman cried again.
"Nay, hasten on — the night is dark
 "And we should search in vain."

— "Oh God! Lord William, dost thou know
 How dreadful 'tis to die?
And can'st thou without pity hear
 A child's expiring cry ?

"How horrible it is to sink
 Beneath the chilly stream,
To stretch the powerless arms in vain,
 In vain for help to scream?" —

The shriek again was heard. It came
 More deep, more piercing loud;
That instant o'er the flood the moon.
 Shone through a broken cloud.

And near them they beheld a child,
 Upon a crag he stood,
A little crag, and all around
 Was spread the rising flood.

The boatman plied the oar, the boat
 Approach'd his resting place;
The moon-beam shone upon the child,
 And show'd how pale his face.

— "Now reach thine hand!" the boatman cried,
 "Lord William reach and save!" —
The child stretch'd forth his little hands,
 To grasp the hand he gave.

<193>

Then William shriek'd; the hand he touch'd
    Was cold, and damp, and dead!
He felt young Edmund in his arms,
    A heavier weight than lead.

The boat sunk down, the murderer sunk
    Beneath the avenging stream;
He rose, he scream'd! — no human ear
    Heard William's drowning scream.

<194>

The Painter of Florence

ROBERT SOUTHEY

PART I

There once was a Painter in Catholic days,[1]
    Like Job, who eschewed all evil;
Still on his Madonnas the curious may graze
With applause and amazement, but chiefly his praise
    And delight was in painting the Devil.

They were angels, compar'd to the devils he drew,
    Who besieged poor St. Anthony's cell;
Such burning hot eyes, such a damnable hue,
You could even smell brimstone, their breath was so blue,
    He painted his devils so well.

And now had the Artist a picture begun,
    'Twas over the Virgin's church door;
She stood on the dragon embracing her son:[2]
Many devils already the Artist had done,
    But this must outdo all before.

---

[1] Southey inserts this epigraph into the poem in his own editions: "The legend of the pious painter is related in the *Pia Hilaria* of Gazaeus; but the Pious Poet has omitted the second part of the story, though it rests upon quite as good authority as the first. It is to be found in the *Fabliaux* of Le Grand." The available translations of LeGrand in English are selections only and do not include this item, and I do not have access to all the volumes of LeGrand in French. A variant of the story-line for Part II, in which Satan undergoes a gender change and is himself the temptress, is recounted in Spooner's *Anecdotes of Painters, Engravers, Sculptors and Architects, and Curiosities of Art*, Vol III, pp. 220-222; Spooner found it in a Spanish art treatise. Lewis would have enjoyed the transvestite Devil much more than the adultery theme in Southey's poem.
[2] Spooner asserts that the painting exists, in "the church of the Holy Virgin at Florence," probably Santa Maria Novella, and then attaches Southey's poem. (217-220). I would appreciate hearing from readers and scholars who can place the LeGrand text or cite the extant painting in Florence.

<195>

The old Dragon's imps, as they fled through the air,
    At seeing it, paused on the wing;
For he had the likeness so just to a hair,
That they came as Apollyon himself had been there,
    To pay their respects to their king.

Ev'ry child, at beholding it, shiver'd with dread,
    And scream'd, as he turn'd away quick;
Not an old woman saw it, but, raising her head,
Dropp'd a bead, made a cross on her wrinkles, and said,
    God help me from ugly Old Nick!"

What the Painter so earnestly thought on by day,
    He sometimes would dream of by night;
But once he was startled, as sleeping he lay,
'Twas no fancy, no dream — he could plainly survey
    That the Devil himself was in sight.

— "You rascally dauber," old Beelzebub cries,
    "Take heed how you wrong me again!
Though your caricatures for myself I despise,
Make me handsomer now in the multitude's eyes,
    Or see if I threaten in vain!" —

Now the painter was bold, and religious beside,
    And on faith he had certain reliance;
So earnestly he all his countenance eyed,
And thank'd him for sitting, with Catholic pride,
    And sturdily bade him defiance.

Betimes in the morning the Painter arose,
    He is ready as soon as 'tis light;
Every look, every line, every feature he knows,
'Tis fresh in his eye, to his labour he goes,
    And he has the old wicked one quite.

<196>

Happy man, he is sure the resemblance can't fail,
    The tip of the nose is red hot,
There's his grin and his fangs, his skin cover'd with scale,
And that — the identical curl of his tail,
    Not a mark, not a claw is forgot.

He looks, and retouches again with delight
    'Tis a portrait complete to his mind!
He touches again, and again feeds his sight,
He looks round for applause, and he sees, with affright,
    The original standing behind.

— "Fool! idiot!" old Beelzebub grinn'd as he spoke,
    And stamp'd on the scaffold in ire;
The Painter grew pale, for he knew it no joke,
'Twas a terrible height, and the scaffolding broke;
    The Devil could wish it no higher.

— "Help! help me! O Mary!" he cried in alarm,
    As the scaffold sunk under his feet.
From the canvas the Virgin extended her arm,
She caught the good Painter, she sav'd him from harm,
    There were thousands who saw in the street.

The old Dragon fled when the wonder he 'spied,
    And curs'd his own fruitless endeavour;
While the Painter call'd after, his rage to deride,
Shook his pallet and brushes in triumph, and cried,
    —"Now I'll paint thee more ugly than ever!"

<197>

PART II

The Painter so pious all praise had acquired,
    For defying the malice of hell:
The Monks the unerring resemblance admired,
Not a lady lived near but her portrait desired
    From one who succeeded so well.

One there was to be painted, the number among,
    Of features most fair to behold,
The country around of fair Marguerite rung;
Marguerite she was lovely, and lively, and young,
    Her husband was ugly and old.

Oh! Painter! avoid her! Oh! Painter, take care!
    For Satan is watchful for you!
Take heed, lest you fall in the wicked one's snare,
The net is made ready — Oh! Painter, beware
    Of Satan, and Marguerite too!

She seats herself now, now she lifts up her head,
    On the Artist she fixes her eyes;
The colours are ready, the canvas is spread,
He lays on the white, and he lays on the red,
    And the features of beauty arise.

He is come to her eyes, eyes so bright and so blue,
    There's a look that he cannot express;
His colours are dull to their quick-sparkling hue,
More and more on the lady he fixes his view,
    On the canvas he looks less and less.

In vain he retouches, her eye sparkles more,
    And that look that fair Marguerite gave:
Many devils the Artist had painted of yore,
But he never attempted an Angel before,
    St. Anthony help him, and save!

<198>

He yielded, alas! for the truth must be told,
    To the woman, the tempter, and fate;
It was settled, the Lady so fair to behold,
Should elope from her husband, so ugly and old,
    With the Painter so pious of late.

Now Satan exults in his vengeance complete,
    To the husband he makes his scheme known;
Night comes, and the lovers impatiently meet,
Together they fly, they are seiz'd in the street,

With Repentance, his only companion, he lies,
    And a dismal companion is she.
On a sudden he saw the old Serpent arise;
— "You villainous dauber,[3]" old Beelzebub cries,
    "You are paid for your insults to me.

"But my too tender heart it is easy to move,
    If to what I propose you agree.
That picture be fair! the resemblance improve,
Make a handsomer picture — your chains I'll remove,
    And you shall this instant be free."

Overjoy'd, the condition so easy he hears,
    "I'll make you more handsome," he said.
He sees that his chain on the Devil appears,
Releas'd from his prison, releas'd from his fears,
    The Painter lies snug in his bed.

At morn he arises, composes his look,
    And proceeds to his work as before:
The people beheld him, the culprit they took,
They thought that the Painter his prison had broke,
And to prison they led him once more.

---

[3] *Dauber*. German word for "painter."

<199>

They open the dungeon — behold in his place,
In the corner, old Beelzebub lay:
He smirks, and he smiles, and he leers with a grace,
That the Painter might catch all the charms of his face,
    Then vanish'd in lightning away.

Quoth the Painter — "I trust you'll suspect me no more,
    Since you find my denial was true;
But I'll alter the picture above the church-door,
For I never saw Satan so closely before —
And I must give the Devil his due."

<200>

Donica

ROBERT SOUTHEY

In Finland there is a Castle which is called the New Rock, moated about with a river of unsounded depth, the water black, and the fish therein very distasteful to the palate. In this are spectres often seen, which foreshew either the death of the Governor, or some prime officer belonging to the place; and most commonly it appeareth in the shape of an harper, sweetly singing, and dallying and playing under the water.

It is reported of one Donica, that after she was dead, the Devil walked in her body for the space of two years, so that none suspected but she was still alive; for she did both speak and eat, though very sparingly; only she had a deep paleness on her countenance, which was the only sign of death. At length a Magician coming by where she was then in the company of many other virgins, as soon as he beheld her he said, "Fair Maids why keep you company with this dead virgin whom you suppose to be alive?" when taking away the magic charm which was tied under her arm, the body fell down lifeless and without motion.

— Thomas Heywood, *The Hierarchies of the Blessed Angels* (1635)[1]

High on a rock, whose castled shade
    Darken'd the lake below,
In ancient strength majestic stood
    The towers of Arlinkow.

The fisher in the lake below
    Durst never cast his net,
Nor ever Swallow in its waves
    Her passing wings would wet.

---

[1] Except for the modernization of spelling to Southey's own time, the epigraph of this poem is a literal rendering of text in Heywood's notes in *Hierarchies of the Blessed Angels* (1635).

<201>

The cattle from its ominous banks
    In wild alarm would run,
Though parch'd with thirst, and faint beneath
    The summer's scorching sun.

For sometimes, when no passing breeze
    The long lank sedges waved,
All white with foam, and heaving high,
    Its deafening billows raved.

And when the tempest from its base
    The rooted pine would shake,
The powerless storm unruffling swept
    Across the calm dead lake.

And ever then when death drew near
    The house of Arlinkow,
Its dark unfathom'd depths did send
Strange music from below.

The Lord of Arlinkow was old,
    One only child had he;
Donica was the maiden's name,
    As fair as fair might be.

A bloom as bright as opening morn,
    Flush'd o'er her clear white cheek;
The music of her voice was mild,
    Her full dark eyes were meek.

Far was her beauty known, for none
    So fair could Finland boast;
Her parents loved the maiden much,
    Young Eberhard loved her most.

<202>

Together did they hope to tread
    The pleasant path of life;
For now the day drew near to make
    Donica Eberhard's wife.

The eve was fair, and mild the air,
    Along the lake they stray:
The eastern hill reflected bright
    The fading tints of day.

And brightly o'er the water stream'd
    The liquid radiance wide;
Donica's little dog ran on,
    And gambol'd at her side.

Youth, health, and love, bloom'd on her cheek;
    Her full dark eyes express
In many a glance to Eberhard,
    Her soul's meek tenderness.

Nor sound was heard, nor passing gale
    Sigh'd through the long lank sedge;
The air was hush'd; no little wave
    Dimpled the water's edge.

Sudden the unfathom'd lake sent forth
    Strange music from beneath,
And slowly o'er the waters sail'd
    The solemn sounds of death.

As the deep sounds of death arose,
    Donica's cheek grew pale;
And in the arms of Eberhard
    The senseless maiden fell.

<203>

Loudly the youth in terror shriek'd,
    And loud he call'd for aid;
And with a wild and eager look
    Gazed on the death-pale maid.

But soon again did better thoughts
    In Eberhard arise,
And he with trembling hope beheld
    The maiden raise her eyes.

And on his arm reclin'd, she mov'd
    With feeble pace and slow,
And soon with strength recover'd, reach'd
    The towers of Arlinkow.

Yet never to Donica's cheek
    Return'd the lively hue;
Her cheeks were deathy white, and wan,
    Her lips a livid blue.

Her eyes so bright and black of yore,
    Were now more black and bright:
And beam'd strange lustre in her face,
    So deadly wan and white.

The dog that gambol'd by her side,
    And loved with her to stray;
Now at his alter'd mistress howl'd,
    And fled in fear away.

Yet did the faithful Eberhard
    Not love the maid the less;
He gazed with sorrow, but he gazed
    With deeper tenderness.

<204>

And when he found her health unharm'd,
  He would not brook delay,
But press'd the not unwilling maid
  To fix the bridal day.

And when at length it came, with joy
  They hail'd the bridal day,
And onward to the house of God
  They went their willing way.

And as they at the altar stood,
  And heard the sacred rite,
The hallowed tapers dimly stream'd
  A pale sulphureous light.

And as the youth, with holy warmth,
  Her hand in his did hold,
Sudden he felt Donica's hand
  Grow deadly damp and cold.

And loudly did he shriek, for lo!
  A Spirit met his view;
And Eberhard in the angel form
  His own Donica knew.

That instant from her earthly frame
  Howling the daemon fled,
And at the side of Eberhard
  The livid form fell dead.

<205>

HENRICUS CORNELIUS AGRIPPA Med & IC.EQU

Nascitur Colon
Agrip 1486
Obijt Anno 1538.

Stemmate natus Eques Medicus Magus atqp peritu

Cornelius Agrippa's Bloody Book[1]

ROBERT SOUTHEY

Cornelius Agrippa[2] went out one day,
His study he lock'd ere he went away;
And he gave the key of the door to his wife,
And charged her to keep it lock'd on her life.

— "And if any one ask my study to see,
I charge you trust them not with the key;
Whoever may beg, and intreat, and implore,
For your life let me only[3] enter that door."

There lived a young man in the house, who in vain
Access to that study had strove to obtain,
And he begg'd and pray'd the books to see,
'Till the foolish woman gave him the key.

On the study table a book there lay,
Which Agrippa himself had been reading that day;
The letters were written with blood within,
And the leaves were made of dead men's skin.

---

1 In his collected poems, Southey changes the title, and adds subtitles and an archaic "moral" at the end of the poem. Southey's final title is "Cornelius Agrippa. / A Ballad, / Of a Young Man that Would Read Unlawful Books, And How He Was Punished." The first stanza is preceded by a subheading that reads, cryptically "Very Pithy and Profitable." Was this an editor's or proofreader's note that slipped into the printed book?

2 Cornelius Agrippa (1486-1535) was an alchemist, occultist and philosopher. His legendary *De occulta philosophia libri tres* (1531-1533) remains a landmark of medieval thinking about the supernatural. In Mary Shelley's *Frankenstein*, Agrippa's book is young Victor Frankenstein's adolescent passion until he discovers modern science with its allure of delivering one of the broken promises of alchemy: to create the *homunculus*, an artificial person. The speechless horror with which the student greets the Devil in this poem parallels young Victor Frankenstein's reaction when first confronted with his own animated monster.

3 Southey changes "me only" to "nobody."

<207>

And these horrible leaves of magic between
Were the ugliest pictures that ever were seen;
The likeness of things so foul to behold,
That what they were is not fit to be told.

The young man he began to read
He knew not what, but he would proceed;
When there was heard a sound at the door,
Which, as he read on, grew more and more.

And more and more the knocking grew,
The young man knew not what to do;
But trembling in fear he sat within,
'Till the door was broke, and the Devil came in.

Two hideous horns on his head he had got,
Like iron heated nine times red-hot;
The breath of his nostrils was brimstone blue,
And his tail like a fiery serpent grew.

— "What would'st thou with me?" the wicked one cried,
But not a word the youth replied;
Every hair on his head was standing upright,
And his limbs, like a palsy, shook with affright.

— "What would'st thou with me?" cried the author of ill,
But the wretched young man was silent still;
Not a word had his lips the power to say,
And his marrow seem'd to be melting away.

— "What would'st thou with me?" the third time, he cries,
And a flash of lightning came from his eyes;
And he lifted his griffin-claw in the air,
And the young man had not strength for a prayer.

<208>

His eyes with a furious joy were possess'd,
As he tore the young man's heart from his breast;
He grinn'd a horrible grin at his prey,
And with claps of thunder vanish'd away.
Henceforth let all young men take heed
How in a Conjurer's books they read.[4]

---

[4] Southey changes the last stanza to read:
   His eyes red fire and fury dart,
   As out he tore the young man's heart;
   He grinned a horrible grin at his prey,
   And in a clap of thunder vanished away.

THE MORAL
Henceforth let all young men take heed
How in a Conjurer's books they read.
—*Westbury, 1798*

<209>

Rudiger

ROBERT SOUTHEY

Divers Princes and Noblemen being assembled in a beautiful and fair palace, which was situate upon the river Rhine, they beheld a boat, or small barge, make toward the shore, drawn by a Swan in a silver chain,[1] the one end fastened about her neck, the other to the vessel; and in it an unknown Soldier, a man of a comely personage and graceful presence, who stepped upon the shore; which done, the boat, guided by the swan, left him, and floated down the river. This man fell afterwards in league with a fair gentlewoman, married her, and by her had many children. After some years the same Swan came with the same barge, unto the same place; the Soldier entering into it, was carried thence the way he came, left wife, children, and family, and was never seen amongst them after.

Now who can judge this to be other than one of those spirits that are named Incubi, says Thomas Heywood[2]. I have adopted his story, but not his solution, making the unknown Soldier not an evil spirit, but one who had purchased happiness of a malevolent being, by the promised sacrifice of his first-born child.

Bright on the mountain's heathy slope
   The day's last splendours shine,
And rich with many a radiant hue,
   Gleam gaily on the Rhine.

---

[1] Opera lovers will instantly recognize this as one of the sources of Wagner's 1850 opera *Lohengrin*. This medieval "Knight of the Swan" folk story, which became part of the French *chanson de geste* tradition, merged with the Arthurian Parcifal legend in Wolfram von Eschenbach's poem *Parzival*, and from thence to the well-known opera. This is the Grail-free version. Southey's "Rudiger" is Eschenbach/Wagner's Lohengrin, a knight of the Holy Grail, who must return home once his identity is revealed, so that his "disappearance" culminates the plot. Wagner adds a pair of Wotan-worshipping villains who are behind the child-stealing and, in his denouement, has the swan return the supposedly-murdered child.

[2] *Heywood.* Southey's source may be the same as the preceding poems (Heywood's *Hierarchies of the Angels* of 1635), but this sounds more like the kind of thing to be found in that author's *Gynaikeion, or Nine Books of Various History Concerning Women* (1624).

<210>

And many a one from Waldhurst's walls
    Along the river stroll'd,
As ruffling o'er the pleasant stream
    The evening gales came cold.

So as they stray'd a swan they saw
    Sail stately up and strong,
And by a silver chain she drew
    A little boat along;

Whose streamer to the gentle breeze
    Long floating flutter'd light,
Beneath whose crimson canopy
    There lay reclined a knight.

With arching crest, and swelling breast,
    On sail'd the stately swan,
And lightly up the parting tide
    The little boat came on.

And onward to the shore they drew,
    And leapt to land the knight,
And down the stream the little boat
    Fell soon beyond the sight.

Was never a knight in Waldhurst's walls
    Could with this stranger vie;
Was never youth at aught esteem'd
    When Rudiger was by.

Was never a maid in Waldhurst's walls
    Might match with Margaret;
Her cheek was fair, her eyes were dark,
    Her silken locks like jet.

<211>

And many a rich and noble youth
    Had strove to win the fair;
But never a rich and noble youth
    Could rival Rudiger.

At every tilt and tourney he
    Still bore away the prize,
For knightly feats superior still,
    And knightly courtesies.

His gallant feats, his looks, his love,
    Soon won the willing fair,
And soon did Margaret become
    The wife of Rudiger.

Like morning dreams of happiness
    Fast roll'd the months away;
For he was kind, and she was kind,
    And who so blest as they?

Yet Rudiger would sometimes sit
    Absorb' d in silent thought,
And his dark downward eye would seem
    With anxious meaning fraught;

But soon he rais'd his looks again,
    And smiled his cares away,
And 'mid the hall of gaiety
    Was none like him so gay.

And onward roll'd the waning months,
    The hour appointed came,
And Margaret her Rudiger
    Hail'd with a father's name.

<212>

But silently did Rudiger
    The little infant see,
And darkly on the babe he gazed,
    And very sad was he.

And when to bless the little babe
    The holy father came,
To cleanse the stains of sin away
    In Christ's redeeming name;

Then did the cheek of Rudiger
    Assume a death-pale hue,
And on his clammy forehead stood
    The cold convulsive dew;

And, faltering in his speech, he bade
    The priest the rites delay,
Till he could, to right health restored,
    Enjoy the festive day.

When o'er the many-tinted sky
    He saw the day decline,
He called upon his Margaret
    To walk beside the Rhine.

— "And we will take the little babe,
    For soft the breeze that blows,
And the mild murmurs of the stream
    Will lull him to repose." —

And so together forth they went,
    The evening breeze was mild,
And Rudiger, upon his arm,
    Pillow'd the little child.

<213>

And many a one from Waldhurst's walls
    Along the banks did roam;
But soon the evening wind came cold,
    And all betook them home.

Yet Rudiger, in silent mood,
    Along the banks would roam,
Nor aught could Margaret prevail
    To turn his footsteps home.

"Oh, turn thee — turn thee, Rudiger,
    The rising mists behold;
The evening wind is damp and chill,
    The little babe is cold!" —

— "Now, hush thee — hush thee, Margaret,
    The mists will do no harm;
And from the wind, the little babe
    Lies shelter'd on my arm." —

— "Oh, turn thee — turn thee, Rudiger,
    Why onward wilt thou roam?
The moon is up, the night is cold,
    And we are far from home." —

He answer'd not, for now he saw
    A swan come sailing strong,
And by a silver chain she drew
    A little boat along.

To shore they came, and to the boat
    Fast leap'd he with the child;
And in leap'd Margaret — breathless now,
    And pale with fear, and wild.

<214>

With arching crest and swelling breast
    On sail'd the stately swan,
And lightly down the rapid tide
    The little boat went on.

The full-orb'd moon, that beam'd around
    Pale splendour through the night,
Cast through the crimson canopy
    A dim discolour'd light:

And swiftly down the hurrying stream
    In silence still they sail,
And the long streamer, fluttering fast,
    Flapp'd to the heavy gale.

And he was mute in sullen thought,
    And she was mute with fear,
Nor sound but of the parting tide
    Broke on the listening ear.

The little babe began to cry,
    Then Margaret rais'd her head,
And with a quick and hollow voice,
    —"Give me the child," — she said.

— "Now, hush thee hush thee, Margaret!
    Nor my poor heart distress;
I do but pay, perforce, the price
    Of former happiness.

And hush thee too, my little babe!
    Thy cries, so feeble, cease:
Lie still, lie still: — a little while,
    And thou shalt be at peace!" —

<215>

So as he spake to land they drew,
    And swift he stepp'd on shore;
And him behind did Margaret
    Close follow evermore.

It was a place all desolate,
    Nor house nor tree was there,
And there a rocky mountain rose,
    Barren, and bleak, and bare.

And at its base a cavern yawn'd,
    No eye its depth may view,
For in the moon-beam shining round,
    That darkness darker grew.

Cold horror crept through Margaret's blood,
    Her heart it paus'd with fear,
When Rudiger approach'd the cave,
    And cried, — "Lo, I am here!" —

A deep sepulchral sound the cave
    Return'd — "Lo, I am here!" —
And black from out the cavern gloom
    Two giant arms appear.

And Rudiger approach'd, and held
    The little infant nigh;
Then Margaret shriek'd, and gather'd then
    New powers from agony.

And round the baby fast and close
    Her trembling arms she folds,
And with a strong convulsive grasp
    The little infant holds.

<216>

— "Now, help me, Jesus!" loud she cries,
   And loud on God she calls;
Then from the grasp of Rudiger
   The little infant falls:

And loud he shriek'd, for now his frame
   The huge black arms clasp'd round,
And dragg'd the wretched Rudiger
   Adown the dark profound.

[Bristol, 1796][3]

---

[3] *Bristol, 1796.* This date and place of composition from the 1838 edition of Southey's poems.

<217>

The Elfin-King

JOHN LEYDEN[1]

— "O swift, and swifter far he speeds
    Than earthly steed can run;
But I hear not the feet of his courser fleet,
    As he glides o'er the moorland dun." —

Lone was the strath[2] where he crossed their path,
    And wide did the heath extend,
The Knight in Green on that moor is seen
    At every seven years' end.

And swift is the speed of his coal-black steed,
    As the leaf before the gale,
But never yet have that courser's feet
    Been heard on hill or dale.

But woe to the wight[3] who meets the Green Knight,
    Except on his faulchion arm[4]
Spell-proof he bear, like the brave St. Clair,
    The holy Trefoil's[5] charm;

For then shall fly his gifted eye,
    Delusions false and dim;
And each unblessed shade shall stand portrayed
    In ghostly form and limb.

---

[1] John Leyden (1775-1811), poet and oriental scholar, whose work includes original poems and translations from Greek, Latin, Hebrew, Persian, Portuguese, and Arabic. He assisted Sir Walter Scott in compiling that author's *Minstrelsy of the Scottish Border*, and contributed to the book's chapter on fairy lore. He also edited the collection, *Scottish Descriptive Poems*.

[2] *Strath*. A wide valley.

[3] *Wight*. Any creature or living being.

[4] *Faulchion arm*. Sword arm.

[5] *Holy Trefoil*. A three-leafed, clover-shaped emblem to ward off evil spirits. As a symbol of the Holy Trinity, it was incorporated into Gothic architecture.

<218>

O swift, and swifter far he speeds
    Than earthly steed can run;
"He skims the blue air," said the brave St. Clair,
    "Instead of the heath so dun.

"His locks are bright as the streamer's light,
    His cheeks like the rose's hue;
The Elfin-King, like the merlin's[6] wing
    Are his pinions of glossy blue." —

— "No Elfin-King, with azure wing,
    On the dark brown moor I see;
But a courser keen, and a Knight in Green,
    And full fair I ween is he.

"Nor Elfin-King, nor azure wing,
    Nor ringlets sparkling bright;"
Sir Geoffry cried, and forward hied
    To join the stranger Knight.

He knew not the path of the lonely strath,
    Where the Elfin-King went his round;
Or he never had gone with the Green Knight on,
    Nor trod the charmed ground,

How swift they flew! no eye could view
    Their track on heath or hill;
Yet swift across both moor and moss
    St. Clair did follow still.

And soon was seen a circle green,[7]
    Where a shadowy wassel[8] crew
Amid the ring did dance and sing,
    In weeds of watchet blue.[9]

---

[6] *Merlin. Falco aeasalon*, a small falcon that hunts in grasslands and moors.
[7] *Circle green*. A fairy circle.
[8] *Wassel*. Drinking and carousing.
[9] *Wachet blue*. A pale shade of blue.

<219>

And the windlestrae,[10] so limber and grey,
    Did shiver beneath the tread
Of the courser's feet, as they rushed to meet
    The morrice[11] of the dead.

— "Come here, come here, with thy green feere,
    Before the bread be stale;
To roundel[12] dance with speed advance,
    And taste our wassel ale." —

Then up to the Knight came a grizly wight,[13]
    And sounded in his ear,
— "Sir Knight, eschew this goblin crew,
    Nor taste their ghostly cheer."—

The tabors[14] rung, the lilts[15] were sung,
    And the Knight the dance did lead;
But the maidens fair seemed round him to stare,
    With eyes like the glassy bead.

The glance of their eyes, so cold and so dry,
    Did almost his heart appal;
Their motion is swift, but their limbs they lift
    Like stony statues all.

Again to the Knight came the grizly wight,
    When the roundel dance was o'er;
— "Sir Knight, eschew this goblin crew,
    Or rue for evermore." —

---

[10] *Windlestrae*. Rye grass.
[11] *Morrice*. A Morris dance, a round dance.
[12] *Roundel*. Roundelay, another Medieval dance.
[13] *Grizly wight*. A person of hideous demeanor, terrifying and otherworldly. By using "wight," Leyden avoids even specifying the speaker's gender.
[14] *Tabors*. Tambourines.
[15] *Lilts*. Cheerful songs.

<220>

But forward pressed the dauntless guest
    To the tables of ezlar[16] red,
And there was seen the Knight in Green,
    To grace the fair board head.

And before that Knight was a goblet bright
    Of emerald smooth and green,
The fretted brim was studded full trim
    With moutain rubies' sheen.

Sir Geoffry the Bold of the cup laid hold,
    With health-ale mantling o'er;
And he saw as he drank that the ale never shrank,
    But mantled as before.

Then Sir Geoffry grew pale as he quaffed the ale,
    And cold as the corpse of clay;
And with horny beak the ravens did shriek,
    And fluttered o'er their prey.

But soon throughout the revel rout
    A strange commotion ran,
For beyond the round, they heard the sound
    Of the steps of an uncharmed man.

And soon so St. Clair the grim wight did repair,
    From the midst of the wassel crew;
— "Sir Knight, beware of the revellers there,
    Nor do as they bid thee do." —

— "What woeful wight art thou," said the Knight,
    "To haunt this wassel fray?" —
— "I was once," quoth he, "a mortal, like thee,
    Though now I'm an Elfin grey. —

---

[16] *Ezlar.* A square hewn stone. Found in the moor, probably a Druid stone.

<221>

"And the Knight so Bold as the corpse lies cold,
    Who trode the greensward ring;
He must wander along with that restless throng,
    For aye, with the Elfin-King.

"With the restless crew, in weeds so blue,
    The hapless Knight must wend;
Nor ever be seen on haunted green
    Till the weary seven years' end.

"Fair is the mien of the Knight in Green,
    And bright his sparkling hair;
'Tis hard to believe how malice can live
    In the breast of aught so fair.

"And light and fair are the fields of air,
    Where he wanders to and fro;
Still doomed to fleet from the regions of heat,
    To the realms of endless snow.

"When high overhead fall the streamers red,[17]
    He views the blessed afar;
And in stern despair darts through the air
    To earth, like a falling star.

"With his shadowy crew, in weeds so blue,
    That Knight for aye must run;
Except thou succeed in a perilous deed,
    Unseen by the holy sun.

"Who ventures the deed, and fails to succeed,
    Perforce must join the crew." —
— "Then brief, declare," said the brave St. Clair,
    "A deed that a Knight may do." —

---

[17] *Streamers red.* The Northern Lights.

<222>

"'Mid the sleet and the rain thou must here remain,
    By the haunted greensward ring,
Till the dance wax slow, and the song faint and low,
    Which the crew unearthly sing.

"Then right at the time of the matin chime,[18]
    Thou must tread the unhallowed ground,
And with mystic pace the circles trace,
    That inclose in nine times round.

"And next must thou pass the rank green grass
    To the tables of ezlar red;
And the goblet clear away must thou bear,
    Nor behind thee turn thy head.

"And ever anon as thou tread'st upon
    The sward of the green charmed ring,
Be no word expressed in that space unblessed
    That 'longeth of holy thing.

"For the charmed ground is all unsound,
    And the lake spreads wide below,
And the Water-Fiend there, with the Fiend of Air,
    Is leagued for mortals' woe." —

'Mid the sleet and the rain did St. Clair remain
    Till the evening star did rise;
And the rout so gay did dwindle away
    To the eldritch dwarfy size.

When the moonbeams pale fell through the white hail,
    With a wan and a watery ray,
Sad notes of woe seemed round him to grow,
    The dirge of the Elfins grey.

---

[18] *Matin chime.* A church bell at daybreak.

<223>

And right at the time of the matin chime
    His mystic pace began,
And murmurs deep around him did creep,
    Like the moans of a murdered man.

The matin bell was tolling farewell,
    When he reached the central ring,
And there he beheld, to ice congealed,
    That crew, with the Elfin-King.

For aye, at the knell of the matin bell,
    When the black monks wend to pray,
The spirits unblessed have a glimpse of rest
    Before the dawn of day.

The sigh of the trees, and the rush of the breeze,
    Then pause on the lonely hill;
And the frost of the dead clings round their head,
    And they slumber cold and still.

The Knight took up the emerald cup,
    And the ravens hoarse did scream,
And the shuddering Elfins half rose up,
    And murmured in their dream:

They inwardly mourned, and the thin blood returned
    To every icy limb;
And each frozen eye, so cold and so dry,
    'Gan roll with lustre dim.

Then brave St. Clair did turn him there,
    To retrace the mystic track,
He heard the sigh of his lady fair,
    Who sobbed behind his back.

<224>

He started quick, and his heart beat thick,
    And he listened in wild amaze;
But the parting bell on his ear it fell,
    And he did not turn to gaze.

With panting breast, as he frowned pressed,
    He trode on a mangled head;
And the skull did scream, and the voice did seem
    The voice of his mother dead.

He shuddering trode: on the great name of God
    He thought, — but he nought did say;
And the greensward did shrink, as about to sink,
    And loud laughed the Elfins grey.

And loud did resound, o'er the unblessed ground,
    The wings of the blue Elf-King;
And the ghostly crew to reach him flew,
    But he crossed the charmed ring.

The morning was grey, and dying away
    Was the sound of the matin bell;
And far to the west the Fays[19] that ne'er rest,
    Fled where the moonbeams fell.

And Sir Geoffry the Bold, on the unhallowed mould,
    Arose from the green witch-grass;
And he felt his limbs like a dead man's, cold,
    And he wist not where he was.

And that cup so rare, which the brave St. Clair
    Did hear from the ghostly crew,
Was suddenly changed, from the emerald fair,
    To the ragged whinstone[20] blue;
And instead of the ale that mantled there,
    Was the murky midnight dew.

---

[19] *Fays.* Fairies.
[20] *Winstone.* A hard rock such as basalt, chert or quartzy sandstone.

<225>

The Sorceress; or Wolfwold and Ulla

[WILLIAM JULIUS] MICKLE[1]

Prisca fides — Virgil[2]

— "Oh, low he lies; his cold pale cheek
    Lies lifeless on the clay;
Yet struggling hope — O day spring break,
    And lead me on my way.

On Denmark's cruel bands, O heaven!
    Thy red-wing'd vengeance pour;
Before my Wolfwold's spear be driven
    O rise bright morning hour!"

Thus Ulla wail'd, the fairest maid
    Of all the Saxon race;
Thus Ulla wail'd, in nightly shade,
    While tears bedew'd her face.

---

[1] William Julius Mickle (1735-1788) was a Scottish poet, now best-remembered as translator of the Portuguese epic *The Luciad*. R.A. Davenport notes Mickle as a ballad writer and says, "Mickle's best composition of this kind is 'The Sorceress' ... which has not often been excelled" (Mickle 19). Sir Walter Scott, in a review, revealed that Mickle was the unattributed poet for 17 spurious ballads in Evans' *Old Ballads* (Scott, *Misc Works* 17, 124). The 1784 edition of Evans mentions Mickle as a contributor, but by the 1810 new edition edited by his son, all mention of Mickle was removed and the ballads were retained (Vol. 4, Nos 15 to 31) with no attribution and with anachronistic language and spelling; Mickle had written imitations of Spenser, so he was adept at this kind of hoax. Davenport accepts this assertion in his 1831 biographical note on Mickle, stating that "he wrote many of the finest pieces in Evans's *Old Ballads*" (Davenport 418). This places Mickle in the same line of work as Lewis, as both translator and fabricator of supernatural ballads.

[2] *Prisca fides*. Found twice in Virgil's *Aeneid*. Book VI, l. 878. "*heu pietas! heu prisca fides!*": "Alas for piety! Alas for the ancient faith!" A less ecclesiastical translation of these words might be "Alas for sense of duty! Alas for simple trustworthiness!" Another use of this phrase is in *Aeneid* Book IX, l. 79: "Prisca fides facto, sed fama perennis": "Ancient is the testimony of the fact, but immortal is its fame." This is more likely what Mickle intends: a claim for reader trust in the narrative.

<226>

When sudden o'er the fir-crown'd hill
    The full orb'd moon arose;
And o'er the winding dale so still,
    Her silver radiance flows.

No more could Ulla's fearful breast,
    Her anxious care delay;
But deep with hope and fear impressed,
    She holds the moonshine way.

She left the bower, and all alone
    She traced the dale so still;
And sought the cave, with rue o'ergrown,
    Beneath the fir-crown'd hill.

Black knares[3] of blasted oak, embound
    With hemlock, fenc'd the cell:
The dreary mouth, half under ground,
    Yawn'd like the gate of hell.

Soon as the gloomy den she spied,
    Cold horror shook her knee;
— "And hear, O Prophetess," she cried,
    "A Princess sue to thee." —

Aghast she stood! athwart the air,
    The dismal screech-owl flew;
The fillet round her auburn hair
    Asunder burst in two.

---

[3] *Knare*. Var. of "knur" or "knar." A knot in the trunk of a tree.

<227>

Her robe of softest yellow, glow'd
    Beneath the moon's pale beam,
And o'er the ground, with yew-boughs strew'd,
    Effused a golden gleam.

The golden gleam the Sorceress spied,
    As in her deepest cell,
At midnight's magic hour she tried
    A tomb o'erpowering spell.

When from the cavern's dreary womb
    Her groaning voice arose,
— "O come, my daughter, fearless come,
    And fearless tell thy woes."

As shakes the bough of trembling leaf,
    When whirlwinds sudden rise;
As stands aghast the warrior chief,
    When his base army flies;

So shook, so stood, the beauteous maid,
    When from the dreary den
A wrinkled hag came forth, array'd
    In matted rags obscene.

Around her brows, with hemlock bound,
    Loose hung her ash-grey hair;
As from two dreary caves profound
    Her blue flamed eye-balls glare.

Her skin, of earthy red, appear'd
    Clung round her shoulder bones,
Like wither'd bark, by lightning sear'd
    When loud the tempest groans.

A robe of squalid green and blue
    Her ghostly length array'd;
A gaping rent, full to the view,
    Her furrow'd ribs betray'd.

<228>

— "And tell, my daughter, fearless tell,
    What sorrow brought thee here;
So may my power thy cares expel,
    And give thee sweetest cheer." —

— "O, mistress of the powerful spell,
    King Edric's daughter see;
Northumbria to my father fell,
    And sorrow fell to me.

"My virgin heart Lord Wolfwold won;
    My father on him smiled;
Soon as he gain'd Northumbria's throne,
    His pride the youth exiled.

"Stern Denmark's ravens o'er the seas
    Their gloomy black wings spread,
And o'er Northumbria's hills and leas,
    Their dreadful squadrons sped.

"— 'Return, brave Wolfwold,' Edric cried,
    'O generous warrior, hear,
My daughter's hand, thy willing bride,
    Awaits thy conquering spear.' —

"The banish'd youth in Scotland's court
    Had pass'd the weary year;
And soon he heard the glad report,
    And soon he grasp'd his spear.

"He left the Scottish dames to weep,
    And wing'd with true love speed;
Nor day, nor night, he stopt to sleep,
    And soon he cross'd the Tweed.

<229>

"With joyful voice, and raptur'd eyes,
    He press'd my willing hand;
— 'I go, my fair, my love,' he cries,
'To guard thy father's land.

" 'By Edon's[4] shore in deathful fray
    The daring foe we meet,
Ere three short days I trust to lay
    My trophies at thy feet.' —

"Alas, alas! that time is o'er,
    And three long days beside,
Yet not a word from Edon's shore?
    Has cheer'd his fearful bride.

"O, mistress of the powerful spell,
    His doubtful fate decide." —
— "And cease, my child, for all is well,"
    The grizzly Witch replied.

— "Approach my cave, and where I place
    The magic circle, stand,
And fear not aught of ghastly face
    That glides beneath my wand." —

The grizzly Witch's powerful charms
    Then reach'd the labouring moon,
And, cloudless at the dire alarms,
    She shed her brightest noon.

The pale beam struggled through the shade,
    That black'd the cavern's womb,
And in the deepest nook betray'd
    An altar and a tomb.

---

[4] *Edon*. Possibly a location on Eden Water, a tributary of the Tweed River.

<230>

Around the tomb, in mystic lore,
    Were forms of various mien,
And efts[5] , and foul wing'd serpents, bore
The altar's base obscene.

Eyeless, a huge and starv'd toad sat
    In corner murk aloof,
And many a snake and famish'd bat
    Clung to the creviced roof.

A fox and vulture's skeletons
    A yawning rift betray'd,
And grappling still each other's bones,
    The strife of death display'd.

— "And now, my child," the Sorceress said,
    "Lord Wolfwold's father's grave
To me shall render up the dead,
    And send him to my cave.

"His skeleton shall hear my spell,
    And to the figured walls
His hand of bone shall point, and tell
    What fate his son befalls." —

O cold down Ulla's snow-like face
    The trembling sweat drops fell,
And, borne by sprites of gliding pace,
    The corse[6] approach'd the cell.

And thrice the Witch her magic wand
    Waved o'er the skeleton;
And slowly, at the dread command,
    Up rose the arm of bone.

---

[5] *Efts*. Lizards.
[6] *Corse*. Corpse.

<231>

A cloven shield and broken spear,
    The figure wander'd o'er,
Then rested on a sable bier
    Distain'd[7] with drops of gore.

In ghastly writhes her mouth, so wide
    And black, the Sorceress throws,
—"And be those signs, my child," she cried,
    "Fulfill'd on Wolfwold's foes!

"A happier spell I now shall try!
    Attend, my child, attend,
And mark what flames from altar high,
    And lowly floor, ascend.

"If of the roses softest red
    The blaze shines forth to view,
Then Wolfwold lives — but Hell forbid
    The glimmering flame of blue!"

The Witch then rais'd her haggard arm,
    And wav'd her wand on high;
And, while she spoke the mutter'd charm,
    Dark lightning fill'd her eye.

Fair Ulla's knee swift smote the ground,
    Her hands aloft were spread,
And every joint as marble bound
    Felt horror's darkest dread.

Her lips, erewhile so like the rose,
    Were now as violet pale,
And trembling in convulsive throes,
    Express'd o'erwhelming ail.

---

[7] *Distained*. Stained.

<232>

Her eyes, erewhile so starry bright,
    Where living lustre shone,
Were now transform'd to sightless white,
    Like eyes of lifeless stone.

And soon the dreadful spell was o'er,
    And glimmering to the view,
The quivering flame rose through the floor,
    A flame of ghastly blue.

Behind the altar's livid fire,
    Low from the inmost cave,
Young Wolfwold rose in pale attire,
    The vestments of the grave.

His eye to Ulla's eye he rear'd,
    His cheek was wan as clay,
And half cut through his hand appear'd
    That beckon'd her away.

Fair Ulla saw the woeful shade,
    Her heart struck at her side,
And burst — low bow'd her listless head,
And down she sunk, and died.

<233>

Bibliography

Allen, John Barrow. *Parnell's Hermit, with Life, Explanatory Notes, Hints for Analysis of Sentences, etc.* 1874. London: Longmans, Green, and Co.

Alliborne, S. Austin. *A Critical Dictionary of English Literature and British and American Authors.* 1858. Philadelphia: J.B. Lippincott.

Anon. *The Anglo-Saxon Chronicle.*

Anon. *A Collection of Old Ballads* [Corrected from the best and most Ancient Copies Extant. With Introductions, Historical, Critical or Humorous]. 1723. London: J. Roberts. [Authorship attrib. to Ambrose Philips (1674-1749).]

Anon. *A Collection of Old Ballads* [Corrected from the best and most Ancient Copies Extant. With Introductions, Historical, Critical or Humorous]. Vol II. 1723. London: J. Roberts. [Authorship attrib. to Ambrose Philips (1674-1749).]

Anon. *A Collection of Old Ballads* [Corrected from the best and most Ancient Copies Extant. With Introductions, Historical, Critical or Humorous]. Vol III. 1725. London: J. Roberts. [Authorship attrib. to Ambrose Phlilips (1674-1749).]

Anon. *Poems of the Elder Edda.* Patricia Terry, trans. (1969) 1990. Philadelphia: University of Pennsylvania Press. [Includes a fine modern translation of "The Waking of Angantyr."]

Axon, William E.A. *The Literary History of Parnell's 'Hermit'.* 1881. London: Taylor and Francis.

Baring-Gould, Sabine. *Curious Myths of the Middle Ages.* Vol 2. 1868. London: Rivingtons. [Discusses "Porsenna, King of Russia" and also has an entire chapter on the legends of Bishop Hatto.]

Barnouw, A.J. *The Making of Modern Holland: A Short History.* 1944. W.W.. Norton & Company.

Bartholin, Thomas [the Younger]. *Antiqvitatum danicarum de causis contemptae a danis adhuc gentilibus mortis libri tres.* (Danish Antiquities on the Causes of the Contempt of Death Felt by The Danish Peoples, in Three Books). 1689. Copenhagen. [With texts in Icelandic and Latin, one source of "King Hakon's Death Song." The original of "The Fatal Sisters," in Icelandic and Latin are on pp. 617-19.]

Brewer, Ebenezer Cobham. *Dictionary of Phrase and Fable.* (1870). Revised by Ivor H. Evans. 1970. London: Cassell & Co.

Brullaughan, Domonick. *Opusculum de Purgatorio Sancti Patritii, Hybernae Patroni. (A Little Work on the Purgatory of St. Patrick, Patron*

<234>

Saint of Ireland) 1735. Louvain: F. Vande Velde. (British Museum, Grenville 4340).

de Bry, Johannes Theodorus. *Florilegium Renovatum et Auctum.* 1641: Frankfurt-am-Main. (Source for illustration of the mandrake root, *Mandragora faemina.*)

Burns, Robert. *The Letters of Robert Burns.* J Logie Robertson, ed. 1887. London: Walter Scott.

————. *Poems, Chiefly in the Scottish Dialect.* Vol. II. 1800. London: Cadell & Davies. [See pp. 195-208 for "Tam O'Shanter."]

Chambers, Robert, ed. *A Biographical Dictionary of Eminent Scotsmen.* Vol III. 1855. Glasgow: Blackie & Son.

Child, Francis James, ed. *The English and Scottish Popular Ballads.* Part I. 1882. Boston: Houghton, Mifflin & Co.

————. *The English and Scottish Popular Ballads.* Part IV. 1886. Boston: Houghton, Mifflin & Co.

————. *The English and Scottish Popular Ballads.* Part V. 1888. Boston: Houghton, Mifflin & Co.

————. *The English and Scottish Popular Ballads.* Part VIII. 1892. Boston: Houghton, Mifflin & Co.

————. *The English and Scottish Popular Ballads.* Part X. 1898. Boston: Houghton, Mifflin & Co.

Collison-Morley, Lacy. *Greek and Roman Ghost Stories.* 1912. Oxford: B.H. Blackwell.

Colman, George, the Younger. *My Night-Gown and Slippers; Tales in Verse.* 1797. London: "Printed for T. Cadell, Jun. and W. Davies."

Costello, Dudley. *A Tour Through the Valley of the Meuse: With the Legends of the Walloon Country and the Ardennes.* Second edition. 1846. London: Chapman and Hall.

Courtney, W.P. "Thomas Lisle." *Notes and Queries.* 10th Series: Nov. 21 1908, 403-04. [Biographical information about Thomas Lisle].

Dasent, George Webbe. *The Story of Burnt Njal, or Life in Iceland at the End of the Tenth Century, From the Icelandic of the Njals Saga.* Volume 2. 1861. Edinburgh: Edmonston and Douglas. [Victorian translation including the poem and framing narrative of "The Fatal Sisters."]

Davenport, R.A. *A Dictionary of Biography.* 1831. London: Thomas Tegg.

Davenport, R.A. "Life of Mickle," in *The British Poets. LXVI: Mickle and Smollett.* 1822. Chiswick: C. Whittingham.

DeLattre, Floris. *English Fairy Poetry: From the Origins to the Seventeenth Century.* 1912. London: Henry Frowde.

Dickinson, A.E.F. "Berlioz's 'Bleeding Nun'." *The Musical Times.* 107:1481 (Jul 1966) pp. 584-588.

<235>

Dodsley, J., ed. *A Collection of Poems in Six Volumes by Several Hands*. Vol 6. 1770. London: Printed for J. Dodsley. [Includes Lisle's "Porsenna, King of Russia" and lines by Pope about Lisle's grotto.]

Dryden, John. *The Sixth Part of Miscellany Poems*. 1716. London: "Printed for Jacob Tonson at Shakespear's Head." [Includes a translation of "The Incantation of Hervor," untitled, with a Latin introductory paragraph, on pp. 387-91. The translator is unattributed, although the poem is in the midst of a group of poems by Richard Corbet, (1582-1635). It seems to have been a random editorial insertion among Corbet's poems. Andrew Wawn states that this is a reprint of Hickes' translation of 1703-05.]

————. *The Works of John Dryden, In Verse and Prose*. Vol. I. 1837. New York: Harper & Brothers.

Edwards, George Wharton. *The Forest of Arden With Some of Its Legends*. 1914 New York: Frederick A. Stokes Company.

Emerson, Oliver Farrar. "The Earliest English Translations of Bürger's Lenore: A Study in English and German Romanticism." *Western Reserve University Bulletins*. xviii:3 May 1915. [Traces the complicated history of the seven different translations of "Lenora" published in 1796.]

Evans, Thomas. *Old Ballads, Historical and Narrative, With Some of Modern Date*. Second edition. 1784. London: T. Evans.

Evans, Thomas, and R.H. Evans. *Old Ballads, Historical and Narrative, With Some of Modern Date*. [A New Edition, Revised and Considerably Enlarged from Public and Private Collections, By His Son]. 1810. London: R.H. Evans

Farley, Frank Edgar. *Scandinavian Influences in the English Romantic Movement*. Studies and Notes in Philology and Literature IX. 1903. Boston: Ginn & Company.

————. "Three 'Lapland Songs'" *PMLA*. 21:1 (1906) 1-39.

Fiske, Christabel Forsythe. *The Tales of Terror*. 1899. Washington, D.C.: The Neale Company.

Fowler, David C. *A Literary History of the Popular Ballad*. 1968. Durham, NC: Duke University Press.

Garlington, Aubrey S. " 'Gothic' Literature and Dramatic Music in England 1781-1802." *Journal of the American Musicological Society*. 15:1 (Spring 1962) 48-64.

Garnett, R. *The Age of Dryden*. 1895. London: George Bell and Sons.

Geyl, P. *The Revolt of the Netherlands (1555-1609)*. 1932. London: Williams & Norgate Ltd.

Gilfillan, George, ed. The *Poetical Works of Johnson, Parnell, Gray, and Smollet, With Memoirs, Critical Dissertations, and Explanatory Notes*. 1855. Edinburgh: James Nichol.

<236>

von Goethe, Johann Wolfgang. *The Poems of Goethe: Translated in the Original Metres*. Edgar Alfred Bowring, trans. 1853. London: J.W. Parker.

———. *The Poems of Goethe*. F.H. Hedge and Leopold Noa, eds. 1882. Boston: S.E. Cassino. [Translation of Goethe by 12 translators, including Bowring, Carlyle, and Longfellow].

Goldsmith, Oliver. The *Miscellaneous Works of Oliver Goldsmith*. Volume 1. James Prior, ed. 1837. London: John Murray. [Includes the essay, "Beauties of English Poetry," commenting on Parnell's poetry.]

Gordon, Alexander. "Taylor, William (1765-1836)." *Dictionary of National Biography*. (1885-1900) Vol. 55. Available online at en.wikisource.org/wiki/Taylor,_William_(1765-1836)_(DNB00)

Le Grand d'Aussy, Pierre Jean Baptiste. *Fabliaux or Tales, Abridged from French Manuscripts of the XIIth and XIIIth Centuries*. G.L. Way, trans. 3 vols. 1815. London: J. Rodwell.

Gray, Thomas. *The Poetical Works of Thomas Gray, With the Life of the Author*. 1782. Edinburgh: "At the Apollo Press." "The Fatal Sisters," pp. 64-8. "The Descent of Odin," pp. 68-72.

———. *The Poetical Works of Thomas Gray*. 1799. London: "Printed for J. Scratcherd." [Includes a literal translation of the original of "The Descent of Odin," showing Gray's omission of the first five stanzas.]

Grose, Francis. *The Antiquities of Scotland: The First Volume*. 1797. London: Hooper & Wigstead. [First printing of Burns' "Tam O'Shanter."]

Gruntvig, Svend. *Danmarks Gamle Folkviser*. (1853).

Guthke, Karl S. "Some Unidentified Early English Translations from Herder's *Volkslieder*." *Modern Language Notes*, 73:1 (Jan 1958) 52-56.

Haller, William. *The Early Life of Robert Southey: 1774-1803*. 1917. New York: Columbia University Press.

Hartman, Geoffrey H. "Wordsworth and Goethe in Literary History." *New Literary History*. 6:2 (Winter 1975) 393-413.

Harvey, Wallace. *Chronicles of Saint Mungo, or, Antiquities and Traditions of Glasgow*. 1843. Glasgow: John Smith & Son.

Herd, David. *The Ancient and Modern Scots Songs, Heroic Ballads, &c.* 1769. Edinburgh: Martin & Wotherspoon. [Expanded to two volumes in 1776. Source for "Clerk Colvill" and "Fair Margaret and Sweet Willliam." Volume II of the 1776 edition includes "Mary's Dream."]

von Herder, Johann Gottfried. *Volkslieder*. (1778-79) 1840. Leipzig: Genhart & Reisland.

———. *Volkslieder*. Part II. (1779) 1911. Munich: Georg Müller.

<237>

Heywood, Thomas. *Gynaikeion, or Nine Books of Various History Concerning Women*. 1624. London: Adam Islip.

Heywood, Thomas. *Hierarchies of the Blessed Angels*. 1635. London: Adam Islip.

Hickes, George. *Linguarum Veterum Septentrionalium Thesaurus Grammatico-Criticus et Archaeologicus*. 1703-1705. Oxford. [6 parts, in 2 vols. I have not seen this volume, and happily cite Andrew Wawn's summary of its contents: "details of saga manuscripts, summaries of saga stories, a supplemented version of Runólfur Jónsson's 1651 Grammar, runic transcriptions and interpretations, and numismatic information." (*Vikings*, 19) "The Incantation of Hervor" appears here in Icelandic and in an English translation, "the first ever published in Britain of a complete Old Icelandic poem" (Wawn, *ibid*, 21)]

Hutchinson, William. *A View of Northumberland, with an Excursion to The Abbey of Mailross in Scotland*. Vol. II. (1776) 1778. Newcastle: Vesey & Whitfield. [First publication of Robert Lambe's "The Laidley Worm of Spindelston Heughs."]

Irwin, Joseph James. *M.G. "Monk" Lewis*. 1976. Boston: Twayne Publishers.

Israel, Jonathan. *The Dutch Republic: Its Rise, Greatness and Fall 1477-1806*. 1995. Oxford: Clarendon Press.

Johnson, James. *The Scottish Musical Museum; Consisting of Upwards of Six Hundred Songs*. Volume V. (1793) 1839. Edinburgh: Wiliam Blackwood & Sons. [Probable source for the version of "Tam Lin" adapted by Lewis.]

Jones, Henry. *Saint Patricks Purgatory, Containing the Description, Originall, Progresse and Demolition of That Superstitious Place*. 1647. London. [Now attributed to Bishop James Spottiswoode.]

Kahlert, Karl Friedrich, and Peter Teuthold. *The Necromancer: Or, The Tale of the Black Forest, Founded on Facts. Translated from the German of Lawrence Flammenberg* (pseud.). 1794. London: Printed for William Lane at the Minerva Press.

Lewes, G.H. *The Life and Works of Goethe: With Sketches of His Age and Contemporaries*. Vol 1. 1856. Boston: Ticknor and Fields.

Lewis, Matthew Gregory. "Giles Jollup the Grave, and Brown Sally Green." *The Spirit of the Public Journals for 1798*. 1:321. 1799 London: James Ridgway.

———. *The Isle of Devils: A Historical Tale, Funnded* [sic] *on an Anecdote in the Annals of Portugal*. 1827. Kingston, Jamaica.

———. *The Monk*. Louis F. Peck, ed. (1796) 1952. New York: Grove Press. [Original text restored, with variant readings.]

————. *Raymond and Agnes; or, The Bleeding Nun.* The Romancist and Novelist's Library. 1841. London: J. Clements.

————. *Tales of Terror and Wonder.* Henry Morley, ed. 1887. New York: G. Routledge & Sons. [includes the spurious *Tales of Terror.*]

————. *Tales of Wonder.* 1801. London: J. Bell

————. *Tales of Wonder.* 1805. Dublin: P. Wogan.

————. *Tales of Wonder.* 1805. Vienna: R. Sammer. [A three-volume edition with many additional poems, including more selections from Percy's *Reliques.* The edition is badly typeset and has a fragment of "Porsenna, King of Russia" in the middle of another poem in Volume III. It is doubtful that Lewis had anything to do with this production.]

————. *Tales of Wonder.* Douglass H, Thomson, ed. 2010. Ontario: Broadview Editions. [A must-read for Lewis scholars. Includes poems I-XXXII, and LVI to LX of *Tales of Wonder,* seven poems from *Tales of Terror,* and extensive notes and excerpts on the critical reception of Lewis's work. Provocative discussion of Lewis, his sources, the confusing print history of *Tales of Wonder,* and the critical issues surrounding parody in these texts.]

Leyden, John. *The Poetical Remains of the Late Dr. John Leyden.* 1819 London: Longman, Hurst, Rees, Orme and Brown.

————. *Scotish* (sic) *Descriptive Poems; with some Illustrations of Scotish* (sic) *Literary Antiquities.* 1803. Edinburgh: Mundell & Son.

Lindsay, Lady. *The Apostle of the Ardennes.* 1899. London: Kegan, Paul, Trench, Trübner & Co., Ltd.

Lockhart, John Gibson. *The Life of Sir Walter Scott.* Vol II. (1837) Abbotsford Edition (Edinburgh Univ. Press). n.d. Boston: Dana Estes & Co. [Details on Scott's correspondence and meetings with Lewis in 1798-99.]

Lynch, Bohun. *A History of Caricature.* 1926. London: Faber and Gwyer.

MacDonald, D.L. *Monk Lewis: A Critical Biography.* 2000. Toronto: Univ. of Toronto Press.

MacQuoid, Katherine S. *In the Ardennes.* 1881. London: Chatto & Windus, Picadilly.

Magnus, Olaus. *Historia de Gentibus Septentrionalibus.* 1555. Rome. [One source for the story of the "Old Woman of Berkeley," including an illustration of her carried off on horseback by the Devil.]

Mallet, David. *Ballads and Songs.* With notes and a Memoir of the Author by Frederick Dinsdale. 1857. London: Bell and Daldy.

Mallet, Paul-Henri. *Introduction à l'Histoire de Dannemarc.* 1755. Copenhagen. [Translated into English in 1770 by Thomas Percy, with many added notes, as *Northern Antiquities.*]

<239>

Malory, Sir Thomas. *Le Morte d'Arthur, or The Hole Book of Kynge Arthur and of His Noble Knyghtes of The Rounde Table*. Stephen A. Shepherd, ed. 2004 New York: W.W. Norton.

Marie de France. *L'Espurgatoire Seint Patriz: An Old French Poem of the Twelfth Century*. Thomas Atkinson Jenkins, ed. 1894. Philadelphia: Press of Alfred J. Ferris. [Complete text of Marie de France's poetic setting of "St. Patrick's Purgatory."]

————. *Saint Patrick's Purgatory*. Michael J. Curley, trans. and ed. 1993. Binghamton: Medieval & Renaissance Texts and Studies Vol. 94. [Side-by-side edition of "Saint Patrick's Purgatory in French and English.]

Mason, Tom. "Dryden's The Cock and the Fox and Chaucer's Nun's Priest's Tale." *Translation and Literature*. 16: Part 1, Spring 2007. pp 1-28.

Mickel, Emanuel J., Jr. *Marie de France*. Twayne's World Authors Series 306: France. 1974. New York: Twayne Publishers Inc.

Mickle, William Julius. *The British Poets*. Vol LXVI: Mickle and Smollett. 1822. Chiswick, C. Whittingham.

Monmouth, Geoffrey. *Historia Regum Britanniae*. (1136).

Nelson, Louise. "The Bokkerijders." Canadian Journal of Netherlandic Studies. 5:2 (1984). [History of the "Goat-Riders."]

Ober, Kenneth H. "Žukovskij's Early Translations of the Ballads of Robert Southey." *The Slavic and East European Journal* 9:2 (Summer 1965) 181-190.

Parnell, Thomas. *Poems on Several Occasions*. Alexander Pope, ed. [Includes "The Life of Dr. Parnell" by Oliver Goldmsith]. 1770. London: T. Davies.

————. *The Poetical Works of Thomas Parnell*. Aldine Edition. [With 1832 "Life of Parnell by John Mitford."] London: Bell and Daldy.

Pausanius. *Description of Greece*. W.H.S. Jones, trans. Vol IV. 1965. Cambridge: Harvard University Press.

Peck, Louis F. *A Life of Matthew Gregory Lewis*. 1961. Cambridge: Harvard University Press.

————. "Southey and Tales of Wonder." *Modern Language Notes*. December 1935. [Asserts that Southey may not have consented to his poems' inclusion in *Tales of Wonder*. Southey's eight poems from the first edition were dropped in the second edition of 1801. Southey's poems do appear in the subsequent 1805 Dublin edition; they are omitted from the 1887 *Tales of Terror* by Morley. Peck appears to mistake Scott's Kelso printing of *An Apology for Tales of Terror* for Lewis's first edition.]

Percy, Thomas. *Reliques of Ancient English Poetry: Consisting of Old Heroic Ballads, Songs, and Other Pieces of Our Early Poets.* Vol I. Fourth Edition. 1794. London: F. & C. Rivington.

——. *Reliques of Ancient English Poetry: Consisting of Old Heroic Ballads, Songs, and Other Pieces of Our Early Poets.* Vol III. Third Edition. 1775. London: J. Dodsley.

——. *Five Pieces of Runic Poetry Translated from the Icelandic Language.* 1763. London: R. & J. Dodsley. [Based upon Verelius and Hickes.]

——. *Northern Antiquities: Or A Description of the Manners, Customs, Religion and Laws of the Ancient Danes.* [Translated from Paul-Henri Mallet's *l'Introduction a l'Histoire de Dannemarc*, etc."] (1770). 1809. Edinburgh: C. Stewart. [This influential volume was reprinted and expanded in 1847 by I.A. Blackwell, and was reprinted numerous times up to the turn of the 20th century.]

Pinkerton, William. "Saint Patrick's Purgatory. Part IV. Modern History." *Ulster Journal of Archaeology.* First series, Vol. 5 (1857), pp. 61-81. [Includes descriptions of St. Patrick's Purgatory, and the Bishop of Clogher's detailed depiction of its destruction in 1632.]

Railo, Eino. *The Haunted Castle: A Study of the Elements of English Romanticism.* 1927. London: George Routledge & Sons Ltd.

Ramsay, Allan. *The Tea-Table Miscellany: A Collection of Choice Songs, Scots and English. (1732-37)* 13th Edition. 1762. Edinburgh: A. Donaldson.

Riely, John C. "Horace Walpole and 'The Second Hogarth'." *Eighteenth-Century Studies* 9:1 (Autumn 1975) 28-44. [Concerning the life and career of Henry Bunbury.]

Robertson, John G. *A History of German Literature.* 1902. New York: G. P. Putnam's Sons.

Roger of Wendover. *Flowers of History, Comprising the History of England From the Descent of the Saxons to A.D. 1235.* [Formerly attributed to Matthew Paris, a.k.a, Matthew of Westminster.] J.A. Giles, trans. (1567) 1849. London: Henry G. Bohn.

Ross, Margaret Clunies. *The Cambridge Introduction to The Old Norse-Icelandic Saga.* 2010. Cambridge: Cambridge Univ. Press. [A definitive overview of Norse-Icelandic sagas, including a fine chapter on the reception of sagas in the 17th to 19th centuries.]

——. *The Old Norse Poetic Translations of Thomas Percy.* Series: Making the Middle Ages, Volume 4, Center for Medieval Studies, Univ. Of Sydney, Australia. 2001. Turnhout, Belgium: Brepols Publishers.

<241>

Scheffer, Johannes Gerhard. *The History of Lapland*. 1674 Oxford: "At the Theatre." [Also, a second, expanded English edition in 1704, with Addenda.]

——. *Lapponia, id est, Regionibus Lapponum et Gentis Nova et Verissima Descriptio*. 1673. Frankfurt. [Original Latin version of *The History of Lapland*, with wood engravings illustrating Lapland customs, pagan religious practices and witchcraft.]

Scott, Sir Walter. *An Apology for Tales of Terror*. 1799. Kelso: "Printed at the Mail Office." Online version by Douglass H. Thomson at www.walterscott.lib.ed.ac.uk/works/poetry/apology/home.html

——. "Copy of An Original Letter by the Late Sir Walter Scott, Bart." *The Lady's Magazine and Museum*. Jan 1837:490. [A letter from Scott to Lewis concerning "Willy's Lady" and several other Scottish Ballads.]

——. "Essay on Imitations of the Ancient Ballad," in *The Complete Works of Sir Walter Scott*. Vol 1. 1833: New York: Cooner & Cooke. [Account of Scott's collaboration with Lewis, and of the publisher of *Tales of Wonder*, pp. 188-89].

——. "Evans's Old Ballads," in *The Miscellaneous Works of Sir Walter Scott*, Vol XVII. 1861 Edinburgh: Adam and Charles Black. 119-136.

——. *Minstrelsy of the Scottish Border*. (1802, 3 vols). One-volume edition. 1869. London: Alex Murray & Son. [First publication of the original version of "Willy's Lady," along with a note about Lewis's version of that ballad for *Tales of Wonder*, pp. 369-72.]

——. *The Pirate*. (Waverly Novels, Volume 23). (1821) 1831. Boston: Samuel H. Parker. [Notes in Volume 1 concerning the oral transmission of the original of "The Fatal Sisters" from the *Saga of Burnt Njal*.]

Scribe, Eugene and Germaine Delavigne. *La Nonne Saglante*. Opera libretto, 1854. Anne Williams, trans. Available online at www.rc.umd.edu/praxis/opera/williams/williams_translation.pdf

Service, James. *Metrical Legends of Northumberland: Containing the Traditions of Dunstanborough Castle, and Other Poetical Romances*. 1834. Alnwick: W. Davison. [Includes notes attempting to connect Lambe's "Laidley Worm of Spindleston Heughs" to historical events and to the struggle between Christianity and paganism in Northumberland.]

Shane, Leslie. *Saint Patrick's Purgatory: A Record from History and Literature*. 1932. London: Burns Oates & Washbourne Ltd. [A compilation of documents about Logh Derg, discussion over the controversy of the "original" cave, and details on the reception and transmisson of the text, including its use by Dante.]

<242>

Skilling, John H. "Auld Nick's View of Alloway." [A detailed traveler's guide to the locales of Burns' "Tam O'Shanter."] Accessed from www.allowaychurch.org/htnl/ourparish.html

Southey, Robert. *Metrical Tales and Other Poems*. 1805. London: Longman, Hurst, Rees, and Orme. [Includes poems that had appeared in *Tales of Wonder*.]

————. *The Poetical Works of Robert Southey*. New Edition. 1845. London: Longman, Brown, Green, and Longmans. [Includes the "Ballads and Metrical Tales" and the preface describing the discovery of the Latin text for "The Old Woman of Berkeley."]

Spooner, Shearjashub. *Anecdotes of Painters, Engravers, Sculptors and Architects, and Curiosities of Art*. 3 vols. 1865. New York: J.W. Bouton.

Stempel, Guido H. *A Book of Ballads Old and New*. 1917. New York: Henry Holt & Co.

Stoupe, J.G.A., ed. *A Collection of Poems by Several Hands*. 1779. Paris: J.G.A. Stoupe. [Includes Lisle's "Porsenna, King of Russia" and Parnell's "The Hermit."]

Sturluson, Snorri. *Heimskringla, or The Lives of the Norse Kings*. Trans. by A.H. Smith, trans. Erling Monsen, ed. (1932) 1990. New York: Dover Books. [Includes the full text of "King Hakon's Death Song" The original edition of this book is *Snorre Sturlessøns Norske kongers chronica* (1633, Copenhagen)].

Torfaeus (Þormóður Torfason). *Ancient History of Orkney, Caithness, & The North*. Rev. Alexander Pope, trans. 1861. Wick: Peter Reid.

————. *Orcades, Seu Rerum Orcadensium Historiae*. 1697. Copenhagen. [One of Thomas Gray's sources for "The Fatal Sisters," in Icelandic and Latin, pp. 36-7.]

Turberville, George. *Epitaphes, Epigrams, Songs and Sonnets, with a Discourse of the Friendly Affections of Tymetes to Pyndara His Ladie*. (1567). c. 1908. London: Henry Denham.

Vedel, Anders Sörensen and Peder Syv. *Et Hundrede udvalde Danske Viser, forögede med det andet Hundrede*. 1695. Copenhagen. [This Danish collection of Icelandic poems contains ballads rather than epic sagas, and is based on Vedel's edition titled *It Hundrede vduaalde Danske Vise* (1591, Ribe).]

Verelius, Olaus. *Hervarar Saga ok Heiðreks Konungs*. (The Saga of Hervor and Heidrekr) 1672. Uppsala. [Swedish with Latin footnotes; the first printed text of this saga.]

Virgil. *Eclogues, Georgics, [and] Aeneid*. Vol 1. H. Rushton Fairclough, trans. 1965. Cambridge: Harvard University Press.

Wann, Andrew. "The Post-Medieval Reception of Old Norse and Old Icelandic Literature." in *A Companion to Old Norse-Icelandic Literature and Culture*. Rory McTurk, ed. 2005. Malden, MA:

<243>

Blackwell Publishing. pp. 320-337. [Detailed chronology of early editions and translations of Norse poetry and sagas.]

————— *The Vikings and the Victorians: Inventing the Old North in Nineteenth-Century Britain*. 2000. Cambridge: D.S. Brewer. [A magisterial survey of the reception of Norse myth and literature, including the publishing history of major source books (Hickes, Percy et al), and the later adoption of Norse themes into poetry and fiction. An indispensible and exhaustive study.]

Warrack, Alexander, comp. *The Scots Dialect Dictionary*. 1911. London: W.R. Chambers.

William of Malmesbury. *Chronicle of the Kings of England*. (1127) John Allen Giles, ed. (1847) 1904. London: George Bell & Sons [A revision of the 1815 translation by John Sharpe. Alternate source for the narrative of "The Old Woman of Berkeley."]

Willson, Anthony Beckles. "Alexander Pope's Garden in Twickenham." *Garden History*. 26:1 (Summer 1998) 31-59.

Wimberly, Lowry C. *Folklore in the English and Scottish Ballads*. 1928. New York: Frederick Ungar Publishing Co.

Wright, Herbert G. "Southey's Relations with Finland and Scandinavia." *The Modern Language Review* 27:2 (April 1932) 149-167.

<244>

About This Book

This book was completely reset from the original 1801 London edition using Aldine type, a face inspired by the designs of the great Venetian humanist printer and publisher, Aldus Manutius. Titles are set in Morris Troy, a typeface designed by William Morris for the Kelmscott Press.

British and archaic spellings, as found in the 1801 *Tales of Wonder*, have been retained for the most part. Repetitive quotation marks within stanzas have been eliminated for esthetic reasons, instead relying on opening and closing quotes for passages. Long dashes, employed by some poets irregularly to separate dialogue, have been added judiciously to help the reader distinguish change of voice.

This book is also available in a PDF ebook edition.

<245>

CPSIA information can be obtained
at www.ICGtesting.com
Printed in the USA
FSOW03n1214120318
45606FS